SWEETER

On the Other Side

Sweet Potato Publishing

For every woman
who longs for true Love

INTRODUCTION

"I think your shirt is inside out."

That's what my hairstylist said to me in the salon, just before draping on the black plastic cape to begin the service that I so direly needed to abracadabra my 1-inch gray roots. The tell-tale sign wasn't just the white tag waving under my armpit, seemingly shouting in sarcasm, "Yup, she's a fashion maverick!" That one indicator of my obliviousness wouldn't have been too bad, even if you add in the seams raggedly running indiscreetly down my sides and arm sleeves.

No, the not-so-subtle clue was most likely the strangely-ornate embroidered spectacle on the front of my shirt. A feisty mob of multi-colored, not-supposed-to-be-seen strings was wrecking havoc on my chest. It was a visual testimony:

This girl's a mess.

But I'm making no apologies.

For the first time ever, I'm learning to accept my seemingly endless flaws. Chuckle at my never-ending mishaps. And feel comfortable in my imperfect skin – regardless of whether my sweater is inside out, I just put my foot in my mouth for the umpteenth time, or the family is grabbing another fast food meal because Mom just can't seem to master this homemade dinner thing. My eyes have been opened to a sweeter way of living – mightier than the mistakes I continue to make daily or the unexpected twists that this life throws at me.

Like when my garage becomes an ice skating rink. I'm dumping a vicious load of homemaker hum-drum ("I didn't sign up for THIS!") on my unsuspecting spouse walking in the door at 6PM. Or my physician calls three days after my usually uneventful annual mammogram with not-so-terrific news.

It's all good.

Because I've discovered the antithesis of Worry. Grumbling. Discontent. Perfectionism. Comparison. Hopelessness. And all other nasty mental detours that previously led me astray from the abundant life.

The remedy?

I'm pursuing an awareness of the presence of Jesus 24/7. Or should I say as much as possible in the ongoing battle between my self-centeredness vs. His Spirit. The more I hang out with Jesus, the more my eyes are fully opened to how only He alone can transform me. As I purposefully look for Him at work all around me – and within me through His Holy Spirit – I find myself finally experiencing Peace. Joy. Contentment. Gratitude. Hope.

And most surprising of all?

The REAL me.

Messy hair, dirty dishes, and all.

I'm still far from perfect. But I do have a perfect Love in my life. And a 100% iron-clad guarantee that His Spirit of Truth living inside me is the key to handling any situation perfectly – both the good and ugly. When I do mess up, Jesus promises to never leave me. There is never condemnation, i.e. "LOSER!! YOU'RE OUT OF HERE!" That, my friend, is the scream of the Enemy.

In contrast, Jesus gently corrects and guides, helping me to be the woman that He created me to be. All the while, He continues to adore me for simply being ME.

How crazy cool is THAT?!

I know, without a smidgen of doubt, that Jesus will never leave me. There is no one else on this planet who can make and deliver on that unshakeable promise.

Have you ever felt completely worthless? Desperately cried out "There's got to be more to this life!" Or ached, and I mean really ached, for a true love that wants nothing more than just to be with you?

My heart's desire is that the Jesus encounters in the following pages will peak your interest, especially if you have not yet personally known His off-the-charts love. Or perhaps your enthusiasm for spending time in God's Word has waned due to the frenzied nature of your now season of life.

Ultimately, my prayer is that you'll be inspired enough by these testimonies of His goodness to set down this book. (That's right, I'm actually advocating my own demise as a writer. Go figure!) Open up THE ONLY BOOK that really matters. And spend quality time with the greatest Love that anyone could ever have the pleasure of enjoying not only today, but after you depart from this world.

God makes it pretty darn simple. He provides only two choices for the love of your life: this world or Jesus. One harshly forces you to conform to unrealistic expectations, which leads to guilt, shame and endless self-blame. The other sets you free to joyfully be who you were created to be.

I choose Jesus.

Shirt inside out. Life upside down. Hanging out with my Savior on "the other side" – a bona-fide heaven even in the midst of residing in a sin-filled earth... where the joy is never-ending and the love oh-so-sweet.

There's no place that I'd rather be.

> This is the real and eternal life: That they know you, the one and only true God, and Jesus Christ, whom you sent.

— JOHN 17:3

WAR OF THE WORLDS

Losing My Religion

I don't want to forget how the Lord rescued me a few hours ago. Typing it up on the keyboard and clicking "Save" just seems to give this experience a bonafide stamp of permanence.

This morning is just another of the endless examples of why setting aside time with Jesus daily isn't a dreaded obligation that I feel required to do out of religious pressure.

I need to connect with my Savior one-on-one for *my very survival* – as a woman, wife and mother. For a *soul-soothing peace* that can't be described in mere words. For a *fresh perspective* – HIS PERSPECTIVE – on what really matters as I try to navigate through this crazy world.

Before I made meeting with the Lord a priority, I'd hit the treadmill to start my day. Or rely on an ultra-hot, singe-the-skin shower to awaken me. Don't get me wrong! These things aren't bad, and I still enjoy them. But only Quiet Time with Jesus has proven to consistently win my ongoing battle between right vs. wrong thinking.

And this morning was no exception.

At 4:30AM, my alarm clock literally screamed. I keep forgetting to change the setting, which seems to have somehow gotten switched from my preferred wakeup via contemporary FM Christian radio.

As a result of my forgetfulness (or likely procrastination which is often my case), I have been rudely awakened the past few mornings to the voice of a male shock jock blaring out the not-always-so-pleasant "news" of the day. The world that we live in – and the media, in particular – seems to focus on the negatives rather than the positives.

Hmm.

Negativity.

I sense a theme here...

I move forward with my daily routine, which begins in bed and under my cozy covers before my feet hit the cold hardwood floor. First, I thank the Lord for *"another day of the gift of life."* Then I praise Him using the A-B-C method: *"Lord, you are Approachable... You are Beautiful... You are Compassionate..."* Basically, I recite 26 of His infinite attributes that just happen to come to mind at that moment – one for each letter of the alphabet. The goal is to reach the letter Z, which seems to always be *"Zealous for your people."* (Any other ideas for Z or X? Please FB message me. And I zealously mean that!)

Truth be told?

I often doze back off around the letter "F," only to be roused by another round of alarming clocks to my sleepy head. After the third or fourth beating – accompanied by a sigh from my once-sleeping hubby – I roll out of bed. But today, for some reason, I decide to get up without the A-B-C's and whack-a-mole-like action on the digital taskmaster to my left.

I sleepily stroll into the kitchen. Fumble for a cup of coffee. *Praise the Lord for the saint who came up with the auto-brew feature!*

Then make way into "my office." Why the quotations? They denote hesitancy for that distinguished title. Much to my horror, The Cat Room is another name thrown out by a visitor to our home, thanks to Potato's litter box in the corner. Evidently not only to human eyes but also nostrils, our feline family member has established dominion over this inspiring author's creative space.

No wonder this book took so long to write.

I proceed to sprawl out on the rug with my Bible. Pray to the Lord for enlightenment, as I always try to do before delving into Scripture. Then start to read Psalm 100[1] with the accompanying commentary from our church's pastor.

≈

Forty minutes later...

I'm convicted that I have not been living "the" life over the past 24 hours. That is, I haven't been the Jesus-focused woman that I'd like to be. Ironically, at the same time that this revelation rocks my spiritual world, I find myself wrestling with earthly distractions – like the housecleaning that is crying out to be my #1 priority; we have out-of-town relatives arriving in a few hours for a weekend visit.

No, they are not staying in The Cat Room.

Plus there's the ever-mounting unanswered emails. Piled on top of that e-mess is the shoulder-crushing reality of training up my two kids, so they hopefully won't walk the same gut-wrenching path as their formally unbelieving mama. We're now one week into summer break, and I still haven't presented my 12-year-old Chase and my 9-year-old Mia with the dreaded "Here's your daily responsibilities" speech and challenge to venture into a deeper relationship with Jesus during the 2½ month vacation from school and our church's youth programs.

Those are just a few icicles forming on the tip of today's "I can't-get-a-handle-on-this!" glacier.

Am I stressed?

No way!

I check Quiet Time off the list. I walk away from my AM date with Jesus convincing myself that I do, indeed, have a renewed God-focused mindset.

Today will be a Kingdom Day!

I proceed into the boudoir.

～

Ok, so our master bedroom is not what one would typically envision to be a dreamy setting for romance. Our king-size bed is covered with Siberian Husky hair. Two large, dust-coated dog crates rest in the corner by the fireplace. And a couple of centuries-old heat pumps clank outside the window nearest to our heads.

Still, it's the only place and time – in the wee hours and darkness of the early morn' – that this couple can find the privacy needed for a personal connection in the midst of raising two tweens who don't like to go to bed early.

I like to follow up Quiet Time by spending an hour with the second most important man in my life (second only to Jesus). Of course, that would be my husband Mike. After our Great Escape, i.e. we lose ourselves in each other for a while ('nuff said), Mike and I pray together while the dogs sound off in their kennels. Perhaps joining in with a canine "Amen."

More likely, it's a beastly cry for breakfast.

After prayer, the day's set into motion. The two of us are off and running into our separate realms of "Senior Director of Global Technology" and "CEO of the Huether Home - Human and Canine Divisions." When the shower turns on, I know that the two hours that I've spent in intimacy, worship and celebration will abruptly end.

Don't misunderstand me! I love the life that God has given me. I try to hang with my Savior 24/7. But the reality? It's so much easier to be joyful and maintain a Christian perspective when I'm alone with Him, lounging on the floor with my Bible in hand, completely focused.

So I digress.

This morning, instead of Mike and I enjoying God's beautiful blessings of one-flesh intimacy between husband and wife, I unintentionally... unexpectedly... uncontrollably lifted up the cap on all my bottled-up worries, frustrations and fears.

Quite simply?

I LOST IT.

It started with me sharing a few sparks of discontent with Mike before our usual hour together, as I walked out of our bathroom and into our bedroom. By the time I slipped under the sheets, I was definitely "hot," but not in the sense of what my hubby envisioned from his usually receptive wife. Basically, my mouth was spewing flames. It was James 3:5-6 in the flesh:

> *It only takes a spark, remember, to set off a forest fire. A careless or wrongly placed word out of your mouth can do that. By our speech we can ruin the world, turn harmony to chaos, throw mud on a reputation, send the whole world up in smoke and go up in smoke with it, smoke right from the pit of hell.*

Yup, that's a Scripture reference.

But it's not one that is giving me kudos for following through with the Kingdom life that I was so committed to pursue after closing my Bible less than 15 minutes ago.

Here's some more irony: Every day or so, I print out a few

words of wisdom from the Book of Proverbs, paired with an interesting visual that I discover via an Internet search. Place the verse with picture on the kitchen counter alongside one of our family's Bibles. Then pray that each member of the Huether clan will be positively moved by the Lord's words of wisdom.

Yesterday's Proverb?

Even a fool who keeps silent is considered wise; when he closes his lips, he is deemed intelligent.

Proverbs 17:28 to be exact, complete with simple imagery of a roll of duct tape. Looks like, in addition to all the other non-Biblical gook that's been piling up (and now gushing violently out of my mouth), Mom is now a hypocrite.

You know what's crazy?

Mike actually listens to me! Time and time again, I'm reminded that the Lord blessed me with the perfect spouse – one that I certainly don't deserve.

～

Forty more minutes later...

Mike graciously endures his supposedly godly wife's tirade. In doing so, he essentially sacrifices his own needs and all possibility of our usual AM intimacy.

Finally, the time has come for the two of us to pray. Mike, bless his heart, covers all the bases – the kids, the visit from relatives, his work. Then he ends with the sweetest observation of his wife's dilemma.

Mike prays that I would see how everything that I'm doing is an opportunity to know and experience God. Every scrub of a toilet. Every push of the lawn mower (but I actually like doing that). Every email that I meticulously write and carefully craft with words of encouragement and complete with a note of Scripture. And those random occasions that this cooking-is-not-my-gift lady actually gets dinner on the table, only to discover that the main entree is a little toasty-looking and crunchy. (Yes, it is possible to burn mac n' cheese.)

After the "Amen" signifying the end of our time together, Mike heads into the bathroom to shave and shower. I walk to the kitchen to dish out breakfast for our canine friends.

Has the prayer worked?

Not exactly.

Just a few minutes after the dogs chow down, I feel that tired-old tormenting inner scream, "WHERE DO I BEGIN??", accompanied by feelings of desperation seeping into my brain. Where do I start on this endless list of unfinished and seemingly "I'VE GOT TO GET THIS DONE TODAY" projects?!

Glancing out the window, I notice one of my dogs reclining peacefully near the very same outdoor table where I sat yesterday. A little less than 24 hours ago, I was joyfully typing away, surrounded by the sights and sounds of His glory, thanks to the majestic countryside that surrounds our home.

Without even thinking – what a blessing! – I grab my coffee cup and computer. *Should I bring anything else? NO!!...* I tell myself... as simplicity seems to be propelling me out the door. I exit the house to join my 10½-year-old Siberian Husky Ben.

Turns out that ol' (canine) man is wiser than me. Because just seconds after I sit down, rather than soaking up the wonder of it all, what's my natural (human) impulse?

"Check your email, Chris."

ARRGGHHHH!!!!

Why do I do this to myself?

Suddenly, the Lord stops me.

I gaze around amazed at a glorious scene similar to the one that I enjoyed yesterday. I beam over a dew-drenched lawn that blazes the most brilliant green... indulge in the sweet sound of hundreds of birds singing, seemingly in harmony, both within my view and hidden in the trees... and marvel at the steamy blanket covering the pond a few yards from my porch.

As I begin to drink up – gulp up is more like it! – this wonderfully divine remedy for my discontent, I notice two geese soaring right toward me... then bee-lining overhead... soon followed by nine others gliding smoothly through the sea of fresh air.

Ahhh....

Thankfulness.

Hey, wait, I think to myself.... then proceed to Google® the very same Psalm that I thought that I was "getting" earlier this morning. I guess that God intended for it to speak to me now...

Now that my heart is right with Him.

And I'm not just going through the Quiet Time motions.

Maybe He knew I wasn't really listening two hours ago. Well, of course, He knew![2] But in His never-ending grace, Jesus continues to pursue me with this message:

Enter my gates with THANKSGIVING.

Somewhere along the way, I LOST IT. I lost perspective of what really matters... and the goodness all around me now.[3] At that moment, Jesus crystalized for me how far I had wandered off the path of contentment, not only this morning but over the past 24 hours...

I was fretting about dirty toilets. Instead, I should have been focusing on the thoughtfulness of my son Chase, who offered to clean the windows for me first thing after he got up yesterday.

I zoned in on the one moment when my daughter Mia said "no" to helping me dust. What I overlooked was how she went outside and gathered flowers for the guest bedroom, picked up her room, and organized her closet (all the clothing arranged by color, no less!). Then she joined me for a walk with the dogs for one of the coolest relational moments of my yesterday.

I dumped on my husband Mike instead of enjoying what precious little alone-time that we have together each day. I could have chosen, instead, to remember all the amazing contributions that he made to our family last night, including making dinner when we ran late at Chase's orthodontist appointment, cleaning up the dishes, and putting up with a chaotic evening after a long day at work.

How does this happen?!

How do I forget God's precious gift of thanksgiving? It's the sure-fire remedy to avoid feeling overwhelmed and becoming the "Chris" that I hated before being transformed by Jesus. It's the only way to "enter His courts"... enjoy His presence... and allow the Holy Spirit to work through me, not just to survive but thrive – whether I'm hanging out alone with Him in the morning... driving down Highway 2 together... or walking alongside Him in my day-to-day activities.

The reality is that His beauty is not confined to my front porch! Thanks to the Holy Spirit, I am in the midst of the beauty of my Creator 24/7 – and that's something that should produce a crazy amount of thanksgiving, Amen?

Nothing is hidden from the Lord. The "old" me found that Truth absolutely terrifying! But after making a commitment to meet with Him every morning, Jesus continues to reveal the beauty of His omniscience (fancy word for all-knowing). Ultimately, it's another facet of His unconditional never-gonna-leave-ya love. Now I like that He sees and knows everything about me! I'm aware that He sees my occasional half-hearted efforts and lapses into negativity.

But instead of leaving me in the pit – where I deserve to be – He reaches down and extends a hand of loving mercy... gently lifting me out and up into His courts – a glorious place free from discontent, ingratitude and self-pity.

It's a slice of paradise here on earth.

Mike, my Godly guy, was right. Thanksgiving is possible in all things. The war of two worlds, Disgruntlement vs. Contentment, has ended. Not because of anything that I have done! Obviously, my lame human efforts at sin management just don't cut it, Amen?

Instead, the victory belongs to Jesus – and how He continues to move me further away from religion into *relationship*. Paradise has been rediscovered with just a little fresh perspective not only from God's Word – a mighty weapon that never fails to knock down my false thinking – but by setting aside alone time with Him daily.[4]

May I forever hold my slightly-scorched oven mitt high!

Or at least until Jesus returns to this earth and brings the whole heavenly pie.[5]

---

1. Shout with joy to the Lord, all the earth. Worship the Lord with gladness. Come before him, singing with joy. Acknowledge that the Lord is God. He made us, and we are his. We are his people, the sheep of his pasture. Enter his gates with thanksgiving; go into his courts with praise. Give thanks to him and praise his name. For the Lord is good. His unfailing love continues forever, and his faithfulness continues to each generation. Psalm 100 (NLT)
2. Even if we feel guilty, God is greater than our feelings, and he knows everything. 1 John 3:20 (NLT)
3. So, my very dear friends, don't get thrown off course. Every desirable and beneficial gift comes out of heaven. The gifts are rivers of light cascading down from the Father of Light. There is nothing deceitful in God, nothing two-faced, nothing fickle. He brought us to life using the true Word, showing us off as the crown of all his creatures. James 1:17-18 (MSG)
4. For the weapons of our warfare are not of the flesh but have divine power to destroy strongholds. 2 Corinthians 10:4 (ESV)
5. ...so also Christ was offered once for all time as a sacrifice to take away the sins of many people. He will come again, not to deal with our sins, but to bring salvation to all who are eagerly waiting for him. Hebrews 9:28 (NLT)

NO THANK YOU

Get A Clue

*W*hy can't I be a better listener?!

Have you ever cried out that question in total frustration, disgusted with yourself, especially when hearing from your child for the umpteenth time: "Mom, I already told you that..." This dagger-thrust-in-a-mama's heart is often followed by a very long adolescent sigh, which – basically – performs as a "YOU DON'T CARE" exclamation mark.

My request to be a better listener has filled one of the top five spots on my prayer list for years. That is, ever since I became a follower of Jesus.

Ouch.

I guess I've been like the clueless sheep that continually wanders off only to be rescued by the Good Shepherd.[1] By rescued I mean that Jesus graciously enables my family to keep loving me despite my moments of drifting off into pastures of stupidity.

Virtually every day, I find myself on my knees pleading with God to help me "live in the moment." This tired-but-true cliché goes hand-in-hand with a commitment to pay attention to all His creations that surround me daily, which can range from stopping to admire this morning's spectacular sunrise to taking a minute to say a few kinds words to the world-weary cashier at the local grocery store.

Why is becoming a better listener so important? In doing so, I value others by putting their interests above my own.[2] I also honor God by showing I appreciate the wonderful people that He has placed in my life.

Sounds so simple.

But what do I actually do?

I find myself succumbing to a barrage of meaningless distractions, which amounts to bad news all-around.

Time and time again, I find myself mentally surveying my To-Do List during a Sunday church sermon... mulling over in my brain what's for dinner while playing with my kids... or mentally walking away during an intimate moment with my husband Mike (which is pretty much equivalent to trashing one of the greatest gifts that Jesus could have ever given to me). What follows these senseless and seemingly uncontrollable incidents is a painful SMACK of GUILTY AFTERMATH. That's in addition to missing out on a great message or conversation. Or worse yet, losing the trust or respect of a friend or family member – creating a devastating emotional injury that can often never be fully repaired.

Why do I DO this?

Why can't I just STOP?!!

I shamelessly confess that it sometimes even happens during my morning Quiet Times with God. Yet He still mercifully forgives me in spite of my sinfulness. Continues to faithfully love me despite my unfaithfulness. And never fails to gently convict me that I can overcome my imperfections through His power and strength... and live out the amazing off-the-charts life that He desires for all His children.[3]

In other words, He gives me glimmers of hope that maybe –

just MAYBE – I can listen more intently and become more like Jesus. Recently, His ongoing message of "Don't quit, I haven't given up on you, Chris" came in the form of pen and paper.

And a left-handed 12-year-old.

~

Two days ago, I asked my son Chase to write a couple of thank you notes.

Chase just returned from a six-day adventure – his first-ever away from home – to a fabulous resort located on one of the most sought-after vacation lakes in the Midwest. He was invited by a classmate and – suffice to say – Chase was blessed with one week filled with never-forget memories, fellowship and character-building moments. Not only did Chase boldly say "Yes!" to the invitation, but he also bravely dabbled in cliff jumping... delightfully reeled in sunfish from a sparkling, glacier-fed lake... relished in late night swims under the stars at the resort's swimming pool... and was treated to Christ-like hospitality from the cabin's owners, his classmate's grandparents.

In my mind, taking five minutes to write a couple of thank you notes – one to his classmate and another to the grandparents – was a small and relatively effortless gesture of gratitude.

Simply put?

It was no brainer.

Guess I was wrong.

The pile of notes remained on the table. Untouched. Finally, I pulled out the big guns of parental warning. Point-blank, I told him – if he wanted to play Xbox® ever again – Chase would need to sit down, pick up a pen, and do the right thing.

That approach did not go over well.

I'm not doing it! You can't make me!

There were other words shared, but you get the point.

I was completely floored. And – to be perfectly honest – absolutely shocked by what seemed to be such a careless attitude towards six days of a good friend plus his family generously pouring out their time... sharing their gifts and treasures... with what appeared to now be an ungrateful young man.

It was hard not to return the harshness.

I praise the Lord for the strength to be still.[4] I remained quiet and calm. I kept reminding myself of Proverbs 19:11:

> *Sensible people control their anger. They earn respect by overlooking wrongs.*

I prayed through every ugly word that floated through my mind seeped with anger... deeply engaged in spiritual battle... thanking the Lord for all the reasons that I love this child... confidently expectant that the Lord would provide.

And He did.

My son shouted out just four words, which – if not mentally on my knees "fighting" with the love and words of Jesus – I may have missed Chase's underlying cry of despair. I likely would have perceived the outburst as hostility or defiance. And if I had chosen the latter path, which was the mantra of my old parenting days, I would have missed an opportunity to see God's mighty work of redemption in my heart.

And my son's.

I'M A TERRIBLE WRITER!

That was Chase's scream.

He was battling insecurity.

My son has struggled with being a leftie in a right-handed world. Ever since he picked up his very first lined paper in Kindergarten, Chase has uncomfortably squeaked out his A-B-C's, his left hand awkwardly crook'd because no one ever taught him how to properly position his paper. I don't blame anyone, as we right-handers just do our thing with little regard to the 10 percent of the population needing a different set of scissors to do something as seemingly simple as cut paper. Wrestling with writing in school notebooks due to spiral binding fighting every move. Bumping elbows at the lunch table every single day.

You get the picture.

All the while, most lefties seem to just grin and bear it.

Up to this point, I was truly unaware of the depth of my son's pain, both physically and emotionally. But God graciously was shining His wonderful light on my darkness.[5] He was showing me that Chase's predicament was a far cry from my previously erroneous notions of laziness or apathy.

Enter the down-the-rabbit-trail response that my kids occasionally venture into... and – sad to say – I often miserably fall for by taking these words personally and, thereby, missing the teaching opportunity.

YOU DON'T LOVE ME!

Again, praise the Lord for providing me – in that moment – with the discipline of silence.

Chase's fountain of insecurity spewed its last ugly drop.

A healing quiet lingered between the two of us.

Finally, Jesus gave me just the right words. In a gentle tone of voice that could only come from my Savior, I explained that if I didn't love Chase, I would get angry. Give up. And walk away. But I loved Chase too much for that tired, old approach.[6]

Again, I became still.

Because I knew that the Holy Spirit would do His thing.

Well, I won't lie and say it was easy. A few drops of frustration were still sprinkled through this "Thank You Cards" project until all was written and done. But after the cards were complete... and Chase walked them out to the mailbox... he returned with a smile and two words that made my heart beam.

Thanks, Mom.

~

From this life experience, Jesus revealed to me that deep within every conversation is buried a CLUE. A revelation of some insecurity. Self-doubt. Feelings of worthlessness. At the root of each of these lies is simply a LONGING TO BE LOVED, because none of us really ever feel good enough. Every one of us is that child who fears rejection – and strives WAY TOO HARD for a perfection that can never be reached.[7]

God's divine love and His Word are the remedy.

Leftie or no leftie.

So I hope that you'll come along with me on this quest to find the hidden message in the next conversation with your child. Your spouse. Your mother-in-law. A good friend.

Or best yet, your worst enemy.

Why not see if you can "get a clue?"

Go beyond the words on the surface and listen for how Jesus may be revealing a desperate need for His everlasting love. By simply honing in non-judgmentally to uncover a person's hidden cry for help, you could be the person that God works through to usher someone into the loving arms of the Savior... not just for an earthly retreat from a moment of discouragement, but a never-gonna-be-cancelled reservation in the most amazing resort imaginable.[8]

Now that's cause for celebration!

You may even get a thank you.

---

1. Jesus said, "If a man has a hundred sheep and one of them wanders away, what will he do? Won't he leave the ninety-nine others on the hills and go out to search for the one that is lost? And if he finds it, I tell you the truth, he will rejoice over it more than over the ninety-nine that didn't wander away! In the same way, it is not my heavenly Father's will that even one of these little ones should perish." Matthew 18:12-14 (NLT)

2. In whatever you do, don't let selfishness or pride be your guide. Be humble, and honor others more than yourselves. Philippians 2:3 (ERV)

3. The thief's purpose is to steal and kill and destroy. My purpose is to give them a rich and satisfying life. John 10:10 (NLT)

4. Be still, and know that I am God! Psalm 46:10 (NLT)

5. But if we walk in the light, as he is in the light, we have fellowship with one another, and the blood of Jesus his Son cleanses us from all sin. 1 John 1:7 (ESV)

6. So let's not get tired of doing what is good. At just the right time, we will reap a harvest of blessing if we don't give up. Galatians 6:9 (NLT)

7. Not a single person on earth is always good and never sins. Ecclesiastes 7:20 (NLT)

8. In my Father's house are many mansions: if it were not so, I would have told you. I go to prepare a place for you. John 14:2 (NKJV)

WANTED

Dead or Alive

A t this moment, I am definitely not in the mood for hanging out in Scripture.

But here I am.

It's 5AM.

I'm clad in the fuzzy pink onesie with detachable feet that my hubby surprised me with this past Christmas. I guess that he finally realized – after 25+ years of wishful thinking – the annual holiday gift of lingerie looks pretty, but doesn't cut it in these Nebraska winters. Bless his heart for cheerfully giving in... and having the confidence that – despite Mom's formless blanket loungewear – our intimate times together can still be exciting.

Really.

SERIOUSLY, they can!

That's what I keep telling myself.

And him.

Once the alarm rings, I step into my giant romper. Wriggle inside and zip up. Then head to a secluded corner of our house for Quiet Time with the Lord. Just Jesus and me, the lady in the oversized Energizer® bunny suit with some serious bed head. Except this morning, something feels different.

The bunny is dead.

Outwardly, my body appears functional. I mean, at least my arms and legs are moving, regardless of their sloth-like pace. I allow my nostrils to lead me safely to my AM fueling station, courtesy of Mr. Coffee®'s auto-brew feature. The dense gonna-put-hair-on-your-chest aroma serves as a traffic guide... guiding this zombie mommie through the pitch-black living room... carefully rounding the corner to avoid kicking the dogs' water bowl... then landing me smack-dab in the kitchen. My hand slowly rises like a bride of Frankenstein to snatch the largest porcelain mug from the cabinet.

Inside, however, I feel completely void of life. Like there's no hope of recharging my 50+ year-old mental battery. Yet I still head to my Quiet Time spot. Get down on my knees. And hope that I'll receive my spiritual fill, so I can tackle the day ahead with the right perspective.

A Jesus perspective.

My head is bowed and arched inward towards my mid-section. Upper body scrunched into a sort of hallowed abdominal crunch. Elbows dug deep into the area rug (which is probably why their rawhide-like exterior could easily be used to scrap loose paint off old furniture).

Hmm.

Adult-sized pink onesie... elbows so roughed up, they could double as hardware restoration tools... throw in this AM's more-than-usual-unruly natural curls... and morning breath seeped in the strongest java possible.

Now I'm thinking, heck! Just give me the coffee can, hand me a spoon and let me dig in. No H20 needed, baby. That's what I call "grounded" in Scripture. LOL.

Back to my less than desirable appearance.

No wonder my hubby has never questioned nor stopped me from leaving our master bedroom at this hour of the morning.

In the Midwest, during the winter months, I experience a double-whammy of goodness during my bowed-down prayer stance. I am not only respectfully worshipping my Savior, but also preserving natural body heat.

I remain humbly facedown. Hunkered low among a few strands of Siberian Husky hair. And perhaps the trace remains of rawhide enjoyed sometime yesterday by my canine family members, Hummer and Redd, in this now sacred space. Like sharp Legos® on a preschooler's playroom floor, the remnants of these natural dog treats pose the danger of embedding themselves into the balls of unsuspecting feet.

I feel the need to insert a "TMI" here.

Too much information, that is, especially if you are not the dog-lovin' kind. In our home, it can be down-right scary at this microscopic level. But I digress into the floor covering.

Back to Jesus, please.

Despite any feelings of lethargy, I know what happens when I faithfully show up every morning in anticipation of meeting my Savior. There's a very real expectation that I'll be swept away – even if just for a moment – by the gentlest voice that I've ever heard into a perfect Kingdom where I am accepted just as I am. Treasured for who He created me to be. Unconditionally welcomed into His holy presence and heavenly family.

Regardless of my childish bedtime attire, which – GULP! – I just realize is legitimately an ultra-hairy-and-scary situation, as I could potentially be mistaken for the controversial hallmark of secular Easter Day tradition, i.e. he has really big ears and often covered in dark chocolate.

This is bad.

Not the chocolate, just the hoppin' imagery.

Guess I'm heading down another you-know-what trail.

More coffee, please!

But maybe a mocha?

Why have I vowed never to miss a morning with Jesus? (That is... in addition to the fact that I appear to seriously need some divine fashion sense.) I meet with Him daily to enjoy a few moments of profound joy from the greatest love relationship that I have ever experienced. That's definitely part of the gift of our get-togethers!

But that's not all.

I DESPERATELY NEED TO BE HERE.

I am often fear-struck with the paralyzing thought that – without my one-on-one AM meetings with Jesus, in addition to meditating on His Word and praying throughout the day – I could easily slip back into the woman that I once was.

And fall into the empty life that I knew not so long ago.

So this is my usual scene before the sun peaks up over the horizon: A hot cuppa joe beside me, overhead lights in the dimmer mode (so as not to wake up the doggies or kiddos), the iPad® app of Bible Gateway® at my fingertips, and my daily devotional in traditional hard-copy style.[1]

Ready and eagerly anticipating being alone with Jesus.

But today feels different.

No matter how hard I try to forget – or move beyond it – I find myself camped out in resentment. Mentally hammered with harsh memories from yesterday. Recalling experiences that, at least at the time that they happened, I *thought* I was handling in a Christ-like way.

Hey, I didn't lose my temper.

I didn't yell or scream.

I was just a little irritated.

Yesterday was one of those days that, from the moment that my kids got into the car after school, the battle lines were drawn. And Mom, alone for the night due to Dad's business dinner with a few out-of-town colleagues, was caught in the crossfire from 4PM until the final prayers were said... after which two war-torn siblings were tucked into their beds by a weary referee.

Now I'm beating myself up.

In those heated moments, why didn't I think to call on Jesus?

Darn that tired-old foe called retrospective.

Truth be told, the Holy Spirit wasn't at work in the laundry room last night when one of my children was arguing with me. In my most "firm not angry" tone, I urged my 9-year-old daughter Mia, who was most certainly thick in the muck of hormonal turmoil combined with friendship strife, to go to her room. RIGHT NOW.

Who am I kidding?!

Let the healthy conviction begin.

Now that I'm hanging out with the One who knows everything, I can see the Light and feel compelled to confess my sins in His loving presence without condemnation.[2] In the laundry room last night, I was feebly employing my own "strength" (to which I add quotations to emphasize the lameness) with the same tired-old strategy: Grit my teeth just enough to get through the moment without "losing it."

I messed up.

Not only that, I was fooling myself into believing that I was operating under the category of "righteousness."

Yikes.

Sorry, Jesus.

Yet, despite my confession, I still can't seem to let go of the bitterness simmering inside me. Before I know it, not only am I mentally boiling over my yesterday's shortcomings, but now today's To-Do List is invading my brain. Ultimately, the Enemy of my soul seems to be successfully tearing me apart from the only One who can save me.

So I pray.

And I PRAY.

And I CONTINUE TO PRAY.

I am TRYING SO HARD to get my thoughts out of this horrible mental dungeon! I can literally FEEL the chains of stubbornness. My state of mind right now is so immersed in negativity, that – when I stop to actually think about what I am doing and feeling – I realize that my eyebrows are scrunched into an unnaturally awkward position that's physically straining! Although I tell myself that I don't want my thinking to stay in this ugly place, I seem unable or unwilling – although it may sound crazy – to free myself from the relentless grip of anger, bitterness and self-pity.

But here I am.

I choose not to leave my prostrated position on the floor, although my prayers seem like lifeless words... void of any intentionality of wanting to do anything but sulk. I am literally in a mental war to prevent myself from falling completely into a black pit of discontent... and definitely fearful that – if I'm not pulled out now – my morning of getting the kids ready before school will not be pleasant.

Oh, Lord, please protect me from the "old days."

Notice the absence of any mention of good.

I'm referring to the days when one of the kids would come down the stairs from their bedroom with that "look" on his or her face. In other words, we're about to see a human time bomb in a countdown mode after being harshly roused by a cruel alarm clock. The potential for widespread damage was very real: just a couple of ill-chosen words accompanied by a nasty tone and facial expression, fired off in the wrong direction, could wipe out all Huether civilization.

One nasty comment could set the entire breakfast scene afire in negativity and virtually guarantee a school tardy... not to mention the gut-wrenching guilt and sadness of a mother glancing back after dropping off a despondent child, red-faced and teary-eyed, in front of the school building.

How did things go so horribly wrong?

Those were the Huether mornings before Mom met Jesus.

My mind is jarred back to the here and now – and into a terrifying WHOA moment. I realize that if I don't change my attitude, this morning's human time bomb would not be one of the kids.

It would be ME.

So here I am.

I look down. See Psalm 33 listed as the next Scripture in my daily devotional. And force myself to read. Although mentally and emotionally, I just don't feel it. And I am definitely not in the mood. Yet I know the Truth:

Jesus is still here with me.

He loves me.

He will never leave me.[3]

Yes, even the presently cranky and unlovable Chris.

So I press on in faith. Power up my iPad. And see The Message version of 1 Corinthians 13:6-7 come up on the dashboard of my digital Bible:

> *If I give everything I own to the poor and even go to the stake to be burned as a martyr, but I don't love, I've gotten nowhere. So, no matter what I say, what I believe, and what I do, I'm bankrupt without love. Love never gives up. Love cares more for others than for self. Love doesn't want what it doesn't have. Love doesn't strut, Doesn't have a swelled head, Doesn't force itself on others, Isn't always "me first," Doesn't fly off the handle, Doesn't keep score of the sins of others, Doesn't revel when others grovel, Takes pleasure in the flowering of truth, Puts up with anything, Trusts God always, Always*

looks for the best, Never looks back, But keeps going to
the end.

WHOA again (but this one is good).

On any other day, I usually just skim the Verse of the Day that pops up... and go my own way through Scripture. But today, Jesus chooses to stop me in my self-deprecating tracks. Extend His glorious hand down into my mental yuck. And lifts me up in the most simple, refreshing and unexpected way.

NOW, I feel it!

It's the wonderfully sensational melting of an icy heart... suddenly overwhelmed in soothing calmness and peace. Although there's really no description, I liken it to immersing in a perfectly warm whirlpool tub... drenching your entire being in a heavenly coziness that can only come from a divine source. My face feels normal again and wrinkle-free. (Well, at least, it *feels* that way. Hey, I'm over 50 and a soon-to-be member of the AARP.[4] All the bitterness that previously enslaved me has vanished, replaced by an empowering Spirit of gratefulness.

That is, the Holy Spirit.

He's living inside of me whether I "feel" it or not. Always present. Forever ready to fight for me... delivering victory in ways that I could have never imagined. I am reignited and reminded of my righteous standing in Christ through just one passage of Scripture. When I first fell to my knees, I was convinced that I would really need to dig deep to get out of this pit. Perhaps plunge myself into an in-depth analysis of Psalm 33.

But not this morning.

Jesus chose to comfort me with just a few profound sentences. Intimately chosen. And perfectly spoken. By Him and Him alone. No commentary needed.

Just for me.

I prepare to shut down my iPad. Now I'm ready not only to

face the day, but jump right into the unknown... convinced that I am totally equipped – *by His strength alone.* And that doesn't mean gritting my teeth the next time that anger threatens to rear its relationship-destructive head. Rather, the Holy Spirit will empower me to fearlessly break through any spiritual barrier that Satan would like to set up to separate me from intimacy with Jesus and my earthly family.

I use to think that my Quiet Time needed to be defined by the clock. One shot of 15 or 30 minutes. Methodically following my own predetermined ritual or one provided by a Bible study. Don't misunderstand me: Bible studies and fellowship are wonderful steps and often necessary, depending on one's season of life. I came to know Christ as my Savior in a Bible study, so I have no gripes.

It's just that for the longest time, I felt that – if I didn't do my Quiet Time "right" – I would not be able to see or hear Jesus. (Yikes! I think that's called legalism.) Ironically, in doing so, I was often so focused on ME that I was listening to the wrong voice.

I was listening to Chris instead of Christ.

BIG difference.

This morning is a refreshing reminder that when God speaks, it may not be exactly how or when I envision. All He asks is that I simply SHOW UP... and be ready to listen to what-ever He wants to tell me. In whatever way He knows that it needs to be said to continue to transform me into His perfect image.[5] All I need to do is be faithful to JUST SHOW UP.

No matter how I feel.

Whatever mood I may be swinging.

So tomorrow morning, I'll be back on my knees, snuggled up in pink fleece from neck to toes, sucking down caffeine before the crack of dawn. And I'll begin with Psalm 33 knowing that Jesus may – or may not – choose to speak to me through that particular Scripture. But what I do know, for certain, is that He will never abandon me. He will always show up with words that remind me of the unfailing Love who breaks through all my fears, weaknesses and ever-changing moods.

Essentially, He wants me.

Dead or alive.[6]

And He wants you, too.

Whether you show up in pajamas, jeans or a business suit.

---

1. Bible Gateway is a searchable online Bible in more than 200 versions and 70 languages that you can freely read, research, and reference anywhere. With a library of audio Bibles, a mobile app, devotionals, email newsletters, and other free resources, Bible Gateway equips you not only to read the Bible, but to understand it. Check it out at https://www.biblegateway.com

2. Nothing in all creation is hidden from God. Everything is naked and exposed before his eyes, and he is the one to whom I am accountable. Hebrews 4:13 (NLT)

3. How blessed the man you train, God, the woman you instruct in your Word, providing a circle of quiet within the clamor of evil, while a jail is being built for the wicked. God will never walk away from his people, never desert his precious people. Rest assured that justice is on its way and every good heart put right. Psalm 94:12-15 (MSG)

4. AARP (formerly the American Association of Retired Persons) is a nonprofit, nonpartisan organization dedicated to helping people ages 50 and older to improve their quality of life as they age.

5. Whenever, though, they turn to face God as Moses did, God removes the veil and there they are – face-to-face! They suddenly recognize that God is a living, personal presence, not a piece of chiseled stone. And when God is personally present, a living Spirit, that old, constricting legislation is recognized as obsolete. We're free of it! All of us! Nothing between us and God, our faces shining with the brightness of his face. And so we are transfigured much like the Messiah, our lives gradually becoming brighter and more beautiful as God enters our lives and we become like him. 2 Corinthians 3:16-18 (MSG)

6. If we are unfaithful, he remains faithful, for he cannot deny who he is. 2 Timothy 2:13 (NLT)

HAPPY NEW YEAR

Sink or Swim

~

This morning, just one day after my two kids returned to school after Christmas break, I am sitting in the Honda® Service Department waiting to hear the cause of the mysterious sound rumbling under our 10+ year-old Pilot. I am feeling remarkably at peace and thanking God... as I reflect on the events over the past three weeks.

~

Shortly before the Christmas, my 4th grade daughter Mia contracted mononucleosis. As a result, she missed the entire last week of school before vacation. The moment that we received the phone call from her pediatrician, I found myself redirecting the traditional holiday cheer to consoling a nine-year-old girl who would miss arguably one of the best weeks of the year.

Darn those once-in-a-lifetime "CAN'T MISS THIS OR I WILL DIE!" classroom parties complete with gift exchanges between classmates and beloved teacher... handmade ornaments that double as keepsakes... and sugar buzzes from over-frosted, sprinkle-drenched cookies and petrified popcorn balls (the culprits behind many-an-elementary tooth loss second only to Laffy Taffy®).

Whether a holiday celebration or spirit theme like Cowboy Day, these buck-the-usual afternoons scream "FREEDOM!" inside every adolescent mind. Elementary boys and girls release their cramped knees from underneath metal desks for the organized chaos of parent-supervised "stations," which likely include some popsicle stick construction and – GULP – glitter glue. If you've volunteered for one of these gigs, you may agree that "supervised" is a word used loosely here. Even if manned by a small army of parent volunteers, I always leave a couple hours later in desperate need of a nap – and in absolute awe of the one person, i.e. teacher, designated to teach this number of kiddos for 180+ days every year.

Why do my kids seem to get sick on the "biggies"? Pajama Day. Library Week. Birthday parties. Those nasty germs don't just afflict their sweet little bodies. With their uncanny timing, these sickening beasts seem hell-bent on attacking their hearts and emotions, too.

For me (a.k.a. Mom), Mia's unexpected medical condition presented a case of missed Christmas activities, but with a slightly different twist. I found myself exchanging home-decorating and card-addressing for dispensing Motrin® and watching movies on the computer screen, cozied up with Mia under the covers of her twin-size bed. I love how God gave us moms the natural instinct to fearlessly care for our young – with no regard for the potential consequences of close encounters of the contagious kind.

Bring it on, Mononucleosis.

After our too-many-to-count $3.99 orders from Amazon Instant Video®, I soon began to realize what this unexpected turn of events really meant (besides a potential phone call from

American Express® alerting me that my account may have been hacked due to a marathon of purchases). That is, I experienced a revelation, but only after a mild, initial panic attack that things this Christmas were not going to proceed as I originally planned.[1] During this transition period from self-focus to God-focus, I could almost feel Jesus lovingly patting me on the back, reassuring me with His always-soothing voice.

It's ok, Chris. It's ok.

I ask myself...

What will I be missing out on anyway?

How about the frantic, last-minute shopping frenzies that follow the discovery – after wrapping what you THOUGHT was the final gift – that big brother has ONE MORE BOX than sis? You know your kiddos are counting, in addition to employing the universal tradition of vigorously shaking every gift package. *(Who determined that violently rattling a once-beautifully wrapped cardboard box would miraculously reveal its contents? And how did this failed method of revelation get passed on through generations?)* And don't you even TRY to stack and wrap a couple of presents TOGETHER in one box to make it look "even-steven." *(I don't know who this "even-Steven" character is, but he is obviously a dreamer who never grasped the reality that life will never be fair. GET OVER IT!)* Our kids are on to that obvious and lame, let's-try-to-keep-the-peace parental scheme.

Then there's the haphazard, assembly-line greeting card production on your kitchen table... complete with a bank-breaking amount of postage stamps... followed by the massive dump into a mail slot at your local post office, which – especially during those *"I've got to get this done today!"* times – is inconveniently located on the other side of town. Not to mention the LLOOONNNNGGG line of disgruntled gift mailers, complete with that ONE PERSON who just can't seem to fill out the paperwork correctly. (That would be me.) Usually, I am rushing out the door to mail our cards on Christmas Eve convincing myself of victory... even though I know that the majority of those cards probably won't make it to their destination until after New Year's Day.

Ho, Ho, Ho.

On a side electronics note, yes, I'm aware of eCard services available. But I'm in the "old school" camp that enjoys opening the mailbox, ripping into the envelope, and oohing-and-aahing over the smiling faces of our friend, neighbors and classmates' families.

Even if I did see the majority of those people in the school hallway yesterday afternoon.

I guess that I can also scratch visitors off my list of any kind or communication with the outside world... due to Mia's medical condition. Although I've been told that mono is not as contagious as other infections, such as the common cold, it seems to carry a stigmatism up there with the likes of strep throat.

Goodbye, world.

Hello, quarantine.

By literally yanking – and I mean that in the most affectionate and loving way – the original To-Do List from my hands, Jesus enlightened me to the truth. This unexpected deviation from my original plan is far from a tragedy, as my enslaving MUST-GET-THIS-DONE ways would have me think. Oh, quite the contrary. Jesus has just blessed me with one of the greatest things that He could have ever given me this Christmas. He is leading me to focus on what really matters... as I ready my heart and our family to celebrate the birth of our Savior.

RELATIONSHIP.

It's funny how I tell myself emphatically... I ALREADY KNOW THIS!

Duh.

Family is one of the greatest year-round gifts that God could ever give me – or anyone for that matter, Amen? Unfortunately, I don't always act in a gracious way to "my people," aka, the Huether clan. Regrettably, that darn pencil and paper with the never-ending checkboxes, i.e, dastardly To-Do List, feels like a ball and chain that can draa-aa-aaa-ggg me through each day.

That is, life becomes a drag if I'm not focused on Jesus daily.

This Christmas, I guess Jesus knew that He'd have to take control, because – quite frankly – I wasn't getting His message earlier. I was getting up every morning and spending time with Him... reading a special devotional related to Christmas... pondering the accompanying Scripture and its application to my life... praying for myself, family and others. But apparently, my listening ears started tuning out around mid-December...

From what I can see now, in retrospect, is that my self-driven holiday goals dressed up in neon-colored Post-It® notes on my office walls were getting the best of me – and threatening my family's entire Christmas – because Mom seemed to be teetering on the edge of insanity vs. singing "God Rest Ye Merry Gentlemen."

Rest being the key word there.

At the time, little did I know that Jesus' gift of quality one-on-one time between Mia and me was just what this schedule-weary mom needed to weather the storms ahead. Mia's mono diagnosis would soon become the least of our holiday surprises.

We ain't seen nothin' yet.

∾

Just a couple of days after Dad and brother Chase officially joined us girls for their respective Christmas breaks, a mysterious sewer-like stench invaded the upper level of our home, which is the location of the kids' bathroom and bedrooms.

The first night that the ominous odor materialized, just around 6PM after dinner (no, it wasn't my cooking this time, thank you), the kids bravely muddled through the foul air during their tuck-ins. Dad successfully convinced them that "it was no big deal." Although my hubby loves our kids, I don't think he relished the idea of sharing our master bedroom.

Go figure.

Interestingly, the smell was gone in the morning.

But as the sun set, I thought I noticed just a hint of the prior evening's offense. One hour later, there was no mistaking it: our respiratory systems were under vicious attack again. The sewer-like pee-yew had quadrupled and intensified to such an extent, it seemed almost certain that our septic system was experiencing its own "I ate too much" after Christmas.

We searched extensively for the source, but to no avail.

The white gas mask was waved. The adults declared defeat. Chase and Mia's steadfast position "We can't sleep upstairs!" proved to be victorious.

Yes, we would all be sleeping in Dad and Mom's bedroom.

Let the celebration begin.

Celebration in the children's minds, I should say. The look on my husband Mike's face communicated his perspective:

This was not on my Christmas list.

This "I guess we have no other option" surrender by the parents was followed by screams of youthful jubilee. Slippery-sock dances on our hardwood floors. Joyful leaps off and on Mom and Dad's king-size mattress. (Insert Dad frown here.) SCRA-A-AA-ATCH! *There went the wood banister.* DOINK! *Hmm... likely a dent in the drywall.* These were among the unsettling sounds generated from seemingly endless hauls up and down the stairs – back and forth – as our children engaged in what seemed to be a relocation of the ENTIRE contents of their bedrooms into ours.

This is for just one night, right?

Mia squeezed all nine of her lovies under our sheets, while strategically placing her no-sew fleece blanket on top of our bedspread. *Your room isn't warm enough.* Me, on the other hand, a premenopausal woman, was sweating already just thinking about it. Dad was busy finalizing the haul and assembly of Chase's twin mattress on the floor next to our bed. Praise the Lord that our two Siberian Huskies remained unfazed by the wretched atmospheric change and remained in their kennels set up in our living room.

Yes, it was a little cramped at first. And I was definitely apprehensive. But much to our surprise, the evening was filled with giggles, heartfelt conversations, and comical make-believe tales, resurrected from the tuck-in days of old from master story-teller Big Daddy. *Lucky the Dog, Muscle Man* and *Silly & Sally* the sock twins were among the original Huether characters who returned from the preschool grave.

The stuff that memories are made of.

Before drifting off to sleep, the four of us joined together in prayer... giving thanks to God for turning a stinky scene into a treasured time that no one could have ever imagined or planned.

Fragrant offering to the Lord?

Hmm.

In our case, Jesus seems to have an interesting "scents" of humor.

∽

The next morning, I carefully peeled the glued-on sheets off my sweaty body... attempting not to awaken the troops... intent on calling the plumber ASAP. First, however, I needed to attend to our two Huskies, whose neglected nails were clanking in their kennels like mental cups on the steel bars of a prison cell.

FOOD AND WATER, PLEASE!

In respect to our canine elder, Hummer (61 years old in human years) is typically the first of our two lovable beasts that I let loose in the mornings. As I unlocked the latch on his kennel, I found myself taken back by the unexpected and disturbing sight before me. My eyes zeroed in on the unthinkable:

A large lump in the center of Hummer's neck.

Strangely, three years earlier, close to this time of year, we had another Siberian Husky, 10½-year-old Ben, who developed a similar lump but positioned near his chest. The size of his lump doubled in size daily, despite numerous visits to our veterinarian in the hopes of a remedy. But alas, it eventually grew to the size of a cantaloupe.

Ben passed away just two weeks later.

Now I found myself staring at Hummer... tears filling uncontrollably and quickly bucketing up in my lower eyelids... and all I could think of to do – beside hold this dog (who is REALLY hungry and needs to urinate BADLY) – is utter these words repeatedly: *Oh, no. Please God. NO....!*

I desperately tried to calm my fears by recalling Bible verses like 1 Peter 5:7:

> *Give all your cares and worries to God, for he cares about you.*

But it wasn't until the rest of the Huether tribe awakened... came out of the bedroom and saw the newest development in this year's increasingly unusual Christmas story... that I became overcome with a sense of contentment.[2] Mike and Chase remained calm and optimistic that the lump was nothing serious. My daughter, Mia, rubbed my back and reminded me:

Trust in the Lord, Mom.

Once again, Jesus transformed crisis into encouragement.

Relationship rules.

And His peace reigns.[3]

∽

pproximately one hour later, for reasons that I don't even remember, I decided to head out to our garage. I didn't need to go out there; because of Mia's mono, Mom and the kiddos were "laying low" with no plans to travel anywhere. Dad had just left in the car about 15 minutes earlier to run an errand.

As I opened the garage door, I was greeted by the surprising scene of what appeared to be at least 2 inches of water swirling around the entire length and width of the cement floor... obviously rising rapidly with each passing minute... along with a thunderous roar like rapids in a whitewater river.

Sloshing through our soon-to-be, unexpected addition of an indoor pool, I discovered the source of the H20 overflow: a pipe under the utility sink in the garage had blown off. Like a garden hose, water was spewing from it, literally by the gallons, flooding the cement floor.

For 15-20 minutes in the coldest winter temperatures that the state of Nebraska had seen for years, my tween son Chase and I worked together to battle our own interior ice storm. Neither of us knew how to shut off the water, so we formed a tag team with 45-gallon totes filling and dumping until Dad returned home to stop the arctic stream. We promptly opened the garage doors and began to sweep the super-sized gray slush out into the driveway.

Two hours later, the cement floor of our garage never looked so clean.

As the outside temps were well below zero for weeks, the Huether's temporarily enjoyed their very own indoor skating rink.

No blades required.

~

Actually, despite the unexpected, our new year did start out quite happy. In the midst of all the strangeness that was unforeseen to us – but not a surprise to our all-knowing God – we found ourselves celebrating His unfailing love, mercy and sovereignty. His Word proved to be the calm in our storms. His presence via the Holy Spirit provided much-needed encouragement, fellowship and strength.

As Christmas break drew to an end, my daughter's mono healed much faster than anticipated. The dog's lump was diagnosed as non-cancerous and, through treatment, was reduced to just an endearing flab of extra skin (a strange reminder of God's saving grace). The stench ended up being an inexpensive fix. And because of God's perfect timing in miraculously leading me into the garage, the plumber ascertained that the flood was likely discovered just minutes after it started. As a result, our family was able to work together quickly as a team to shut it down, preventing costly damage to any of the contents in our garage.

As we reflected on those crazy days, our family marveled and praised Him for each and every rescue. We also reminded ourselves that – when we don't freak out – we get the privilege of seeing first-hand His glorious grace in action. Experience contentment in all situations. And share these miracles with others as a testimony to His everlasting love and faithfulness.

Even when life gets truly stinky.

However, I must confess.

I'm praying this doesn't become a holiday tradition.

≈

Back here in the Honda service department, I was just informed by the mechanic that our Pilot's brakes were nearly non-functional... and that – due to the timing of stopping in right now – I avoided certain disaster on the road. It's the same vehicle that our family had been driving throughout Christmas break, from grocery trips into town to late night drives out in the middle of nowhere to see the brightest of holiday lights.

And guess what?

This morning, I didn't have an appointment scheduled for the vehicle. I just felt God's prompting that something just wasn't quite right... followed His lead to 27th Street and Yankee Hill Road... then enjoyed the blessing of knowing – without doubt – that my Savior is always with me.

Praise the Lord.

The One who adds the "happy" to every new year.

Jesus helps you walk on the water.

Even when your garage becomes a raging sea.

---

1. We can make our plans, but the Lord determines our steps. Proverbs 16:9 (NLT)
2. You keep in perfect peace all who trust in you, all whose thoughts are fixed on you! Isaiah 26:3 (NLT)
3. And let the peace that comes from Christ rule in your hearts. For as members of one body you are called to live in peace. And always be thankful. Colossians 3:15 (NLT)

THE WORD

On 98th Street

"What's another word for 'anxious'?" I asked the student.

"Excited?" she replied.

"How about 'worried'?" I suggested. Then I visually demonstrated by pretending to bite my fingernails accompanied by the statement: "I'm so nervous about my test today!"

Earlier this morning, I had the privilege – once again – of listening to the 4th graders recite their weekly verse at the faith-based school that my two children attend. I also get to ask the students to share the meaning of that particular Scripture. That's what I consider the proverbial icing on the cake of being the volunteer Bible verse listener – hearing how God's Word is speaking to these young hearts and minds in the students' own words. There is nothing sweeter than words of Life coming from the mouths of babes.

I memorize the verse, too, along with my daughter Mia. This week's verse was the NIV version of Philippians 4:6:

Do not be anxious about anything, but in every situation, by prayer and petition, with thanksgiving, present your requests to God.

Regardless of whether a child sails through the verse or stutters along, I know any investment in memorizing Bible passages brings blessings.[1] That's why on Friday mornings, my heart beats wildly 23 times, i.e. the number of kids in Mia's class. As I listen to absolute Truth coming from each student's mouth – and look deeply into his or her eyes – I know the verse will come to life to make His presence known in a very real way, somewhere at just the perfect time preordained by the Lord Himself.

I can offer proof.

Philippians 4:6 played out for me vividly two hours ago.

$\sim$

"Do you mind staying just a few minutes later than usual?" Mia's 4th grade teacher kindly asked, as I hit the halfway mark of students who had recited their verses. She wanted to take the kids outside in the snow, which was quickly developing into blizzard-like conditions. The kids were scheduled to take a test on precipitation later that morning... and she was tickled that the Creator of the Universe would bless them with a first-hand look, taste and feel of His own homemade white slush.

No problem, I replied.

As the class began gleefully tumbling out the room into the hallway, the teacher called "Come along with us, Mrs. Huether!" I followed but hung back in the foyer of the Elementary building, watching from a distance as the kids jumped for joy on God's big dance floor of snow. They were having the time of their lives.

The snow was starting to make me jumpy, too. But, unfortunately, joy is not an adjective that I would use to describe my jitters. Philippians 4:6 came to my mind, and I chuckled to myself – and shot up a look at my best friend Jesus. "Do not be anxious about anything...." I said under my breath, while looking at the snow and thinking of the 25-minute drive back home on Highway 2. The Severe Weather Alert issued earlier that day was becoming a reality before my very eyes.

And so was my daughter's verse.

After what seemed much longer than I'm sure it really was due to my trepidation about the pending trip home, a gang of totally jiggly 9 and 10-year olds were sliding their way back down to the classroom. I took my place in the hallway and finished hearing the words, "Do not be anxious..." repeated over and over again.

I finished listening to the last child. Entered the classroom to give my favorite verse reciter (Mia) our traditional hug-and-kiss before leaving for the morning. And said to Mia's teacher with a smile, "I might be needing this verse for the drive back home!" Outwardly, I believe that I spoke these words as a show of confidence.

Inside, I felt my usual post-Bible verse cheer waning slightly.

~

A s I exited the parking lot, my Honda Pilot® spun out just a bit.

"Do not be anxious about anything...." I muttered to myself. At that moment, despite the slide, I realized that instead of my usual panic attack... I was not frightened! *Thank you, Jesus.* I turned on the radio... let out a sigh... and continued down the road in awe of how the weather forecasters appeared to have gotten it right this time.

Don't get me wrong; I am not slamming meteorologists. I think that they have one of the toughest jobs on the planet. It seems tough because, ultimately, God is in control despite all the technology. If He wishes the wind to change direction, it will do an about-face. Or maybe He desires to stir up a snowstorm after a sunny morning in March. He created the Universe, right? So certainly, He can tell it what to do!^{2}

Back inside the vehicle, I WAS FEELING GOOD driving down 98th Street! Yes, it didn't LOOK good with the snow definitely now coming down in buckets (or should I say shovels). I even let out a chuckle as I effortlessly passed the HVAC repair truck that was driving down the left side of the road at a turtle pace. This is really not so bad after all, I told myself. I was giddy that I was driving with God-confidence, as – just a few years before or maybe even months – I would have been paralyzed with fear in similar conditions.

I headed toward the traffic light, which marked my left turn from 98th Street onto Highway 2.

Oh, I WAS FEELING GOOD! Although I wasn't rocking out in the vehicle full force, I was swaying back and forth to the tune of "God's Great Dance Floor" by Chris Tomlin... reflecting on how I was joyfully dancing in my car seat now – in blizzard condition, no less – because of Him.

The light turned green. I moved toward the intersection. Looked to my right and – in what seemed like slow motion – saw a mini van in the far righthand side failing to stop. YIKES! I pressed on my breaks... and started to slide uncontrollably. My car began to turn... and I could see that I would miss him.

PRAISE THE LORD!

A split second later, however, I saw that – on my left side – A SEMI TRUCK was now gliding towards me. In my previous euphoria, I failed to notice this 20,000 lb. monster in the traffic mix. My car was now positioned dead-center of the intersection, the proverbial sitting duck, with no way to make a quick exit.

My eyes zoned into the driver's horrified face, as we both seemed to silently communicate: *This is not going to end well.* I frantically kept turning the wheel, hoping for a miracle... but I found myself seemingly destined for my demise. Then, as if a mighty invisible hand swooped down, the 10-ton beast was miraculously shoo'd slightly to the left... sliding a mere three feet alongside me. The semi continued to slide through the intersection... without hesitation (traction, that is)... onward into the city of Lincoln. My car rested just inches from the median.

I quickly realigned myself. Gave the accelerator a few pushes, eventually dislodging my SUV. Turned onto the highway. And headed down the icy road towards home... praising the Lord. Thanking Him that – until my preordained time comes – I can be confident that He will keep me safe.

"Do not be anxious about anything..."

∾

R ight now, I'm sitting in my cozy living room by the fireplace. Typing this story for His glory. A story about how His Word always delivers results. He always speaks the Truth. And He is my everlasting Savior. Not just here in my house.

But also on the corner of 98th and Highway 2.

The rest of the drive home earlier today? Not bad at all! Because the Truth of His Word kept ringing joyfully in my ears. But I did keep the radio turned off. And my knuckles, well, let's just say that the color has returned after a 20-minute vice grip.

Here's the amazing thing, though. In just a few seconds, I'll be shutting down the computer and heading back down that icy road to retrieve my kiddos. And, yup, it's still snowing. No doubt, the road conditions have taken a turn for the worse. But just as I tell myself every Friday morning when meeting with those sweet students reciting verses, I know that hiding His Word in my heart is one of the most priceless things that I can do![3] More times than I could ever mention, my commitment to memorizing Scripture has proven to be THE KEY to getting me through some of the greatest life challenges.

So I will dust the snow off my car hood. Take a deep breath. And know with 100% assurance that I have nothing to fear, because He will save me again – if not later today or later this week – on the day that I take my last breath and ascend to my final destination.[4]

I am so thankful that I have invested time in knowing and understanding His Word, not only by listening to those precious 4th graders but also compiling my own memory verses. Because when I do, He always brings just the perfect words to mind to give me a supernatural peace unlike anything of this world. This morning, He kept me level-headed in a crisis situation that could have killed me, if the old Chris – infamous for panicking and freaking out – would have been behind the wheel.

And that's a mighty powerful return that no earthly investment can ever deliver.[5]

Do I hear an Amen?

Or perhaps a Philippians 4:6.

I will definitely be reciting it with meaning again in just a few minutes when I turn the ignition to start my second drive into Lincoln. And perhaps so should a very relieved semi driver somewhere out there on the other side of Highway 2.

"Do not be anxious about anything..."

---

1. Study this Book of Instruction continually. Meditate on it day and night so you will be sure to obey everything written in it. Only then will you prosper and succeed in all you do. Joshua 1:8 (NLT)

2. I know the greatness of the Lord—that our Lord is greater than any other god. The Lord does whatever pleases him throughout all heaven and earth, and on the seas and in their depths. He causes the clouds to rise over the whole earth. He sends the lightning with the rain and releases the wind from his storehouses. Psalm 135:5-7 (NLT)

3. Oh, how I love all you've revealed; I reverently ponder it all the day long. Your commands give me an edge on my enemies; they never become obsolete. I've even become smarter than my teachers since I've pondered and absorbed your counsel. I've become wiser than the wise old sages simply by doing what you tell me. I watch my step, avoiding the ditches and ruts of evil so I can spend all my time keeping your Word. I never make detours from the route you laid out; you gave me such good directions. Your words are so choice, so tasty; I prefer them to the best home cooking. With your instruction, I understand life; that's why I hate false propaganda. Psalm 119:97-104 (MSG)

4. I tell you the truth, those who listen to my message and believe in God who sent me have eternal life. They will never be condemned for their sins, but they have already passed from death into life. John 5:24 (NLT)

5. Every word of God proves true. He is a shield to all who come to him for protection. Proverbs 30:5 (NLT)

GOTCHA!

It's in the Cards

When I meet face-to-face with Jesus in Scripture, I'm always struck by how He enlightens me with a fresh perspective.

Sometimes, His sweet whispers of Truth are actually accompanied by a physical sensation of His presence. It literally feels like He jumps out of the page embracing me with a supernatural hug. I liken this experience to the two disciples on the road to Emmaus in the Gospel of Luke.[1]

Yup.

It's THAT good.

No self-help book, TV show or podcast comes even close.

Other times, I experience a sickening feeling in my stomach as the stark contrast between His goodness and this sin-saturated world is painfully revealed. That's when I start to think, "I've got to stop reading the national news during my lunchtime!" Fortunately, Jesus never bolts from the scene leaving me in a state of hopelessness. Oh no, quite the contrary. That's one of the many extraordinary qualities about my Savior. Only Jesus has a way with words that can lift anyone – and I mean ANYONE – out of depression or paralyzing fear. Speaking from personal experience, I can tell you that His encouragement can only be described as DIVINE.

There are also times when Jesus brings to light something – something shockingly ugly – unconsciously hidden within me. Thankfully, revelations like this from Jesus never feel like a scolding. There's no condemnation.[2] Just a gentle conviction that restores so beautifully.

That's how I know it's the voice of Jesus.

Although initially taken back that I previously failed to realize this sin inside of me, I'm quickly overcome by an overwhelmingly positive sense of RELIEF. Why? Because there is no harsh judgmental tone that often taints even the most genuine effort of mere mortals to "speak the truth in love." On the contrary, the Son of God discloses my sinfulness with a tenderness like no other. His indescribably forthright yet utmost caring approach always draws me closer and makes me a better person.

It almost certainly marks the beginning of another possibly uncomfortable yet necessary step toward becoming more like Him.[3] That's one of the many reasons why I look forward to my daily hour with Jesus so desperately.

Admittedly, however, I'm not always prompt to show up every morning. I still have to push the snooze button at least twice. (Ok, my first confession of the day: THAT'S A LIE.) I'm typically suffering from a major case of bed head. (I blame my naturally curly locks sprinkled with a few grey wiry stragglers.) And I've taken on the disguise of a freakishly large raccoon, courtesy of day-old mascara smeared under tired 50+ year-old eyes. Too wiped last night to wash my makeup away.

In other words, this ain't looking pretty.

But Jesus is still waiting.

Always glad to see me.

~

This morning, I'm reading Psalm 38, which was penned by King David under the divine guidance and inspiration of God.[4] I sense He's prompting me to pause at David's gut-wrenching personal testimony in verses 17 and 18:

> *For I am ready to fall, and my sorrow is continually before me. For I confess my iniquity. I am full of anxiety because of my sin.*[5]

Right now, I don't see how this particular Scripture applies to me. But I feel that, for some reason, the Lord may be telling me that I am not praying fervently enough for my family.

Ok, I agree with that.

So what's a naturally performance-driven gal who has struggles with letting the Lord totally lead do?

I set aside the Psalm. Head into our home office to retrieve a stack of index card cards that I haven't used in ages. Return to my cozy spot with Jesus. And start to write out what I am calling a "prayer card" for each member of the Huether clan, starting with my 13-year-old son.

CARD #1: CHASE

The first thing that pops in my head?

BIBLE STUDY

I can feel the tension already.

You know, when one or both eyebrows start to uncomfortably scrunch... and even the natural pull from gravity can't seem to keep them at ease?

Currently, Chase and I are reading through Proverbs together before bedtime. Well, it's more like I'M reading it, while he playfully coaxes (headlocks is probably a better description) our feisty Siberian Husky Redd into reclining next to him.

Chase and I have enjoyed some amazing Bible times together. But, as of late, we are definitely in a lull.

WHEW.

I'm so glad that the Lord led me to pray about what to do with this kid!!

AMEN!

ORGANIZATION & FOLLOW-THROUGH

This one really gets my heart beating. *Sorry, Lord...* I find myself confessing... *Bible study is definitely the #1 priority, but this topic kind of trips my trigger.*

Trips my trigger?

I just realize that doesn't sound very Biblical.

Chase is an incredibly smart young man. He definitely knows more than his mother at the age of 13. In fact, it blows my mind how he rarely brings schoolwork home; my son definitely takes after his dad (not mom) in the ability to retain information with just a glance or two.

So how is it that – while Chase maintains an "A" average in every subject – he just happens to forget a paper or project once or twice every quarter? The end result is that Chase's once-hard-sought-after "A" promptly tumbles down into a let's-settle-for-less "B." Now, a "B" is still good, don't get me wrong! But when you KNOW that the kid can do better, well...

MYSTERIOUSLY IRRITATING!

That's the gentlest way I can describe it.

When I ask "Why, dude? WHY?" Chase says he simply forgot... or the paper just got misplaced in one of two black holes of junior high: his locker or backpack. I mean, do these two regions of academic space have a gravitational pull so intense that no matter or radiation (or paper due the last week of the quarter) can escape becoming infinitely lost inside?!

Then it start hits me.

Bible study. Organization. Follow-through.

Who are we talking about here?

OH, NO.

Here it comes.

I don't think this prayer card is for Chase...

GULP.

Perhaps I have taken a nonchalant approach lately to my kid's nighttime Bible study. Maybe I've become lazy. Or mentally shut down around 6PM due to an exhausting day. I've been justifying my lackadaisical attitude with a *"Why doesn't CHASE come up with the next study?!"*

OUCH.

The proverbial fog has lifted.

I realize that I'm "THE ONE."

I'd resolved myself to stay in a lifeless mode. Making no effort at all to change things. Using the excuse that I'm "waiting on the Lord."

Yah, RIGHT.

So I'm partly at fault for letting our mom-son Bible team down. And when was the last time that I actually followed-through with my cleaning plan? I mean... tumbleweed-size canine hairballs are rolling around our hardwood floor. And have I organized a strategy for dinner? If it's like last night, I will be defaulting to leftover mac n' cheese and past-their-prime carrot sticks so bendy that they put Gumby® to shame.

Then I hear it.

GOTCHA :-)

Ok, maybe that's the Message version. And I'm not sure if God uses emojis, but I'm going with it.

I'm sensing that Jesus is saying to me something along the lines of Matthew 7:1:

*Do not judge others, and you will not be judged. For you will
be treated as you treat others. The standard you use in
judging is the standard by which you will be judged.*

It's that darn "being judgmental" thing!! Except instead of
logs in the eye, we're talking wilted celery sticks from the refrig-
erator of a woman who is in dire need of some fresh veggies,
thanks to procrastinating on that weekly grocery trip.[6]

Shall we continue?

How many times have I asked the kids to pick up their bathroom counter... when the kitchen counter is full of Mom's clut-
ter? I justify this double standard by telling everyone that I am
the "House Manager." I NEED to have my calendar – and stacks
of "to do" piles – on the counter to visually remind me of what's
"really important."

YIKES.

That has now officially become my word of the day.

Caps included.

~

D id I fill out a "prayer card" for the rest of my family
members, e.g. Dad and Mia? Yes, I did. But no need to
share the gory details. (Or should I say "glory" details,
because I'm so very glad that God revealed my sinfulness!)

The end result was the same.

When I spread all my cards, i.e. sins, out on Jesus' table, I
was playing a losing hand.[7] It was the game of judging others,
while overlooking my own shortcomings.[8]

Insert GASP here.

If I hadn't taken time out this morning to meet with Jesus, I
would have most certainly continued down this finger-pointing
path. No doubt, my destructive thinking and accompanying

behavior could have done some serious damage to the three earthly relationships that are most precious to me... not to mention my spiritual relationship with the One who loves me more than anything.

He even died for me.[9]

So what's a humbly convicted gal who sees the errors of her ways to do?

She gets down on her knees. Confesses her sins. Thanks the Lord for His love and mercy. And vows to let the Holy Spirit instill in her the patience, humility and Christ-like compassion to forgive others and move forward in love.[10]

I now realize that it's 6:17AM.

I'm still in my pajamas with my Bible, still open to Psalm 38, spread out on the carpet in front of me. No progress in the areas of personal care, shower and makeup. The table above me (I'm a floor dweller) has become the pedestal for my mountain of used Kleenex®. (Ok, so I cried a little.) And I haven't gotten past verses 17 and 18!

But it's all good.

Because when I confess my sins to Him, God is faithful and just! He forgives my sins and cleanses me from all wickedness.[11] In other words, He wipes my slate clean.

Or should I say, erases the scribbles on the "prayer cards"?

Prayer cards?

Yah, right.

Crazy thing is, I know that even if I pull another piece of 3x5 file card from the drawer – in other words, RELAPSE! – the Lord will once again lovingly come alongside me, like a Father helping his toddler firm up those wobbly steps to avoid a disasterous header into self-destruction. And together, hand-in-hand, we'll be walking steadily through His Word again. With a little tumble here. And a slip up there.

Because HE is that good!

So very good to a Christ-following toddler like me.
See you tomorrow morning.[12]
No file cards needed.

---

1. That same day two of Jesus' followers were walking to the village of Emmaus, seven miles from Jerusalem. As they walked along they were talking about everything that had happened. As they talked and discussed these things, Jesus himself suddenly came and began walking with them. Luke 24:13-15 (NLT) *Read in your Bible through to verse 35 for the whole amazing story!*
2. The Lord will redeem those who serve him. No one who takes refuge in him will be condemned. Psalm 34:22 (NLT)
3. You were taught to leave your old self. This means that you must stop living the evil way you lived before. That old self gets worse and worse, because people are fooled by the evil they want to do. You must be made new in your hearts and in your thinking. Be that new person who was made to be like God, truly good and pleasing to him. Ephesians 4:22-24 (ERV)
4. All Scripture is given by God. And all Scripture is useful for teaching and for showing people what is wrong in their lives. It is useful for correcting faults and teaching the right way to live. 2 Timothy 3:16 (ERV)
5. Psalm 38:17-18 (NASB)
6. Jesus said, "And why worry about a speck in your friend's eye when you have a log in your own? How can you think of saying to your friend, 'Let me help you get rid of that speck in your eye,' when you can't see past the log in your own eye? Hypocrite! First get rid of the log in your own eye; then you will see well enough to deal with the speck in your friend's eye." Matthew 7:3-5 (NLT)
7. You spread out our sins before you – our secret sins – and you see them all. Psalm 90:8 (NLT)
8. If we claim we have no sin, we are only fooling ourselves and not living in the truth. 1 John 1:8 (NLT)
9. But Christ died for us while we were still sinners, and by this God showed how much he loves us. Romans 5:8 (ERV)
10. Most important of all, love each other deeply, because love makes you willing to forgive many sin. 1 Peter 4:8 (ERV)
11. 1 John 1:9 (NLT)
12. Seek the LORD and His strength; seek his face continually. 1 Chronicles 16:11 (ESV)

TRAVEL ADVISED

It's A God Thing

T he dreaded "What if".

These two words have been a constant roadblock on my spiritual journey. Why is it that a mere six letters can wreck major havoc inside my heart and mind? That's the question the Lord leads me to ponder this morning, as I meditate on Psalms 42 and 43.

Spoken aloud or internally, the phrase "what if" doesn't just slow me down from moving forward. It literally acts as a mental time bomb, igniting my smallest (and often unsubstantiated) fears into an all-out explosion of anxiety that ruins any chance of the joy that Jesus desires for me.

This morning, I find myself tempted to revert to my pre-Jesus doomsday mentality, triggered by the words "what if," which – in the past – have left me paralyzed in fear.

Next week, our family of four will venture out of the country together for the first time. At this moment, I'm feeling pretty darn uncomfortable about it! I hate that feelings of insecurity – everything that has to do with travel, especially for more than three days away from home – are relentlessly poking around in my thought life, as our date of departure approaches.

What if we get separated from one of our kiddos in the airport? Our dogs get mistreated at the kennel? Our home is broken into or a water pipe bursts while we're gone? (Hey, two of three aforementioned scenarios have actually happened to our family, just to show that I'm not too far off the paranoid charts!)

Someone is attempting to sidetrack me from the excitement that I'd been enjoying over past few months, while planning and anticipating eight days of sun, fun and adventure during our upcoming Mexico vacation. Thankfully, the more time I spend in God's Word, the better I'm able to distinguish between two voices that battle for my attention daily: the Truth and the Liar.[1] The Bible says that it's a spiritual battle.[2]

A few years ago, after a number of previous attempts, I finally read through "The Screwtape Letters" by C.S. Lewis in its entirety.[3] It was quite the accomplishment for me, because I had started diving into this classic many times only to stop midstream. Why so difficult to finish? I found myself taken back – ok, more like frightened – by the truth that Satan is real! Of course, I knew this fact before reading it. But the imagery in this C.S. Lewis book? You just have to read it for yourself to understand the power behind what is often referred to as a literary masterpiece.

One of the realities shared in "The Screwtape Letters" is Satan's diabolical strategy for sucking the joy out of God's children: cleverly duping us into pondering the "what if's." If we fall for this too-far-ahead thinking, it keeps us nervously on edge like soldiers in a war zone, constantly looking out for landmines, i.e. calamities, that likely don't even exist!

Mental landmines is what they feel like to me. What they really do is keep me from "living in the moment." This morning, the Liar seems deviously intent on not just thwarting all celebration about my upcoming vacation. Oh, I'm sure that's part of it!

But even more disturbing, I feel that the Enemy is attempting to wreck havoc on my Quiet Time with Jesus.

I take another look at Psalms 42 and 43. Then I think a little more about the Psalmist. He started his "Quiet Time" with the Lord by being completely honest, even if that meant throwing out a few "what if's" to wrestle with together.

I used to think that it was sacrilegious to throw up any question to God that began with those two words. I recall that members of a former Bible study said doing so was sinful, that I was not trusting in the Lord. *(Hmm. I believe that's called legalism?)* I was also advised not to shoot up any "why?" in a gut-wrenching prayer... because I would then be doubting that God works all things together for the good of those who love Him.[4] So I kept the "what-if's" and "why's" buried inside of me... even though those words – and all the emotions piled up along with them – were on the verge of boiling over. Funny thing is... Jesus knows exactly what I'm thinking whether I say it aloud or not.[5] *(That, my friends, is what I believe is called irony.)*

So why not simply ask Him?

Why not wrestle through the stuff of life... from the smallest details to the potential life-changers... with the God of the Universe, my best friend? I give kudos and thank you to the Psalms for enlightening me that – honestly – I'm not questioning His goodness! I'm simply acknowledging that I can do nothing without Him. He is completely in control of the past, present and future.

And I can rest in that.

Huh.

I do believe that God works all things together for our good! I know that this trip is God's plan for our family. Everything fell into place so perfectly. Now Jesus has me thinking: Why not transform the formerly evil "what if's" into some gloriously good thoughts?

What if God is using this trip not solely for our enjoyment, but He's also laying the foundation for a greater purpose in our lives? A Huether child moved by compassion to become a missionary? Or perhaps a few strangers along the way will become friends, thanks to acts of Christ-like kindness?

Good-bye, self-focus and doubt.

Hello, Psalms 42 and 43!

This morning, this remarkable chunk of Scripture opened my eyes, once again *(yeah, I need lots of reminders, but Jesus knows that and it doesn't bother Him a single bit)* to see the triple-whammy of God's goodness:

He loves me.

He never lies.

I can trust Him.

I love how Psalm 42:5, in the Message version, sums up how God is always ready to listen to whatever I bring Him: *Why are you down in the dumps, dear soul? Why are you crying the blues? Fix my eyes on God – soon I'll be praising again. He puts a smile on my face. He's my God.* I can chat with Him about anything and everything – and I mean EVERYTHING – confident that He listens, loves and advises me perfectly.

Yup, He's my God!

Plus my travel advisor.

And that's good to know right now.

Because my news-lovin' hubby just texted me – as I step away from the warm glow of the fireplace and His comforting words until we meet again tomorrow morning – that one of Mexico's most notorious drug lords was just apprehended in none other than guess what place?

The Huether's vacation designation.

I still trust Him!

But would it be ok to pack my pepper spray?

---

1. He (Satan) was a murderer from the beginning. He has always hated the truth, because there is no truth in him. When he lies, it is consistent with his character; for he is a liar and the father of lies. John 8:44 (NLT)

2. For we are not fighting against flesh-and-blood enemies, but against evil rulers and authorities of the unseen world, against mighty powers in this dark world, and against evil spirits in the heavenly places. Ephesians 6:12 (NLT)

3. Lewis, C. S., April 21, 2015, *The Screwtape Letters*, New York: HarperOne; Reprint edition

4. And we know that God causes everything to work together for the good of those who love God and are called according to his purpose for them. Romans 8:28 (NLT)

5. You know what I am going to say even before I say it, Lord. Psalm 139:4 (NLT)

HOMESICK
Paradise Found

It's 1:15AM.

After tossing and turning for over 1/2 hour in the king-sized bed of our master suite, I find myself alone on the living room floor wrapped in one of four signature robes provided by our 5-star luxury resort, tucked away in obscurity off the coast of Mazatlán, Mexico.

Our villa is over 2,600 square feet, the size of a primary residence back in the States, complete with a full kitchen and laundry room. Exquisitely carved 12-foot doors open into an open-air foyer complete with an endlessly-flowing, blue-illuminated fountain.

The sheer size of the living room alone is enough to make any jaw hit the floor. But it's also outfitted with a sliding glass door that spans over 40 feet across the length of one wall. This grand exit leads to our family's private pool (at least for the next 7 days) aligned with multi-colored strobe lights complete with Jacuzzi, encased by tropical bushes bursting with blazingly-colored flowers and overlooking a golf course designed by a renowned golf pro.

Oh yeah, and this dreamy scene is bordered by a stunning mountain range.

This view into a seemingly paradise on earth is unobstructed, that is, with the exception of a choppy visitor. Smack dab in the middle is a helicopter port. Just a few hours ago, someone had apparently used it to have clothes flown into the resort. As the copter landed, several young bellhops scurried to the door under the moving blades to retrieve two things: a pair of trousers and a shirt.

That's one heck of a return trip from the dry cleaners.

We later heard that these esteemed articles of clothing were rumored to be owned and flown in by one of the country's governing officials, who was staying in the resort's executive suite.

My son Chase and daughter Mia are currently tucked away in their own ornately-decorated bedrooms with sky-high ceilings; each of their spacious digs includes its own widescreen plasma TV and floor-to-ceiling windows. Each room comes complete with a private bathroom decked out with an oversized glass-encased shower with never-ceasing hot water flowing from a Frisbee®-sized head. I know for a fact that we have no hot water issues, as my son was lost in this simulated tropical waterfall for about 2 hours.

Shortly thereafter, void of all skin elasticity, Chase was asked by the restaurant maître d' if he'd like to take advantage of the resort's Senior Discount.

Apparently, he was mistaken for an 80-year-old retiree.

Ok, that's an exaggeration.

But I feel like I am smothered in excesses right now from the caged peacocks and scantily-dressed Greek statues embellishing the resort lobby to the winding sidewalks bordered by coconut trees, waterfalls and koi-stocked pools complete with flamingos and lizards.

Yes, these creatures are real, moving parts and all.

I can't sleep.

But it's not due to the local lizards, which we've been told, fall from the trees.

My stomach feels like it's now at the top of my throat. At first, I thought the queasiness could be attributed to the $7 pumpkin and shrimp soup that I ordered earlier off the room service menu. It's hard to tell whether this ill feeling is due to the rich soup base or exorbitant cost, which I will undoubtedly regret when I see the final food bill.

Who am I kidding?

I know this nausea isn't physical.

In other words, it's not tummy troubles.

It's definitely the sign of a troubled heart, courtesy of a few Psalms that I've been reading and mediating upon during our stay, which speak to the seemingly never-ending chasm between the poor and the prosperous.

I'm feeling pretty darn uncomfortable right now.

My 9-year-old daughter feels it, too. Last night, our first night in "paradise," Mia was in tears because there was nothing at the $25 per person buffet that appealed to her simply satisfying peanut butter sandwich lifestyle. She also sadly told me that – even after swimming all afternoon in her "own" pool – Mia missed her friends and cozy country home.

I realize just how deeply now that I miss it, too.

Yes, I'm feeling grateful for our blessings back home. I long to be tackled and exasperated by our playful Siberian Husky, Redd, who can't sit still for a minute and likes to "affectionately" ram his head between your legs. I feel sad that later today, Mia and Coach Mike (aka Dad) will miss the cheers, dribbles and giggles from a dozen 4th grade girls at their last basketball game of the season. And I pray that our home hidden away on a secluded county road in the boonies remains left alone and trouble-free.

But mainly, I'm wondering if this unsettling sensation may be something along the lines of conviction.

I am drowning in hypocrisy.

Troubled by the injustice I see.

Yet wading waist high in an effervescent private Jacuzzi.

I'm still confident that this vacation was a "God thing." I mean, all the logistics of this trip just came together way too perfectly. In my own strength, no matter how much research and energy invested, I simply could not have pulled off this great Huether adventure.

It started with an email four months ago from a friend who co-owns the timeshare and was offering it up to anyone who would like to use one of her weeks. Remarkably, the cost per night was around the same that we'd pay to stay overnight in a hotel in Kansas City. Throw in the fact that the school calendar was virtually activity-free (with the exception of the basketball game), in addition to Mike's work schedule. Then top it off with the miraculous thumbs up from Delta® that – YES! – Mike could use his frequent flyer miles to purchase four tickets and fly into Mazatlán at just the right dates with perfect flight times.

As the icing on the vacation cake, after we booked the resort and flights, my friend thoughtfully mailed me a five-page overview of all the cautions and joys of staying in this particular timeshare, as well as traveling broad. She even threw in two maps of the area, as well as dining and activity suggestions.

The Huether's don't usually indulge in the once-a-year big vacation like many other families. Left on my own, I cringe at spending thousands of dollars in one shot. And my feeble mind is simply unable to pull off all the specifics, from scheduling to packing to planning activities. (Twenty-five years ago, my husband and I opted to elope to Las Vegas versus a year or more of wedding planning. Nuff said!) That's why our family of four has previously engaged in only one other major cross-country trek three years earlier. I felt that trip to Southern California was God-ordained, too, fueled by frequent flyer mile redemption, coupons and a friend's thoughtful advice.

It's a God thing!

That's what I told myself three years ago when God beautifully orchestrated that first B-I-I-I-G family vacation. And now, those were the same words that I repeated again here in Mazatlán, chuckling with Mia when a man named Jesus opened the mammoth wrought iron gates at the end of a majestic driveway aligned with tropical trees. (That was his name, I kid you not.) He gave the universal thumbs up signal to our airport shuttle driver, an official "Go ahead, you've been approved for entry" when we arrived earlier today.

It's a God thing!

That's what we all agreed when.... travel-weary, hungry, confused by the pesos thing and struggling to temporarily acclimate ourselves into a different way of life... the waiter at poolside came to our table and noticed our dumbstruck condition. He held up his wrist, graced with a salvation bracelet, which was the EXACT MATCH as the one worn daily by my husband Mike. Then our brother in Christ from across the border, thankfully also an English-speaking one, kindly showed us how to order and pay for our late 2:30PM lunch.

It's a God thing!

Yes, I know that He was walking alongside us. I had no doubt that our safe travels and other countless blessings on the way were delivered at the hands of our great Provider.[1] It's just that – up until this sleepless night – I failed to see another lesson that He's trying to teach me.

And it wasn't pretty.

Earlier today, as we made the 30-minute shuttle drive from

the airport to the resort, our family drove through one of the most poverty-stricken areas that I've ever seen. Not one building was free from graffiti. Broken-glass windows on stone-crumbling homes were meagerly sheltered with ripped sheets. Shirt-torn and shoeless men, women and children of all ages gathered outside on old couches around broken card tables amid garbage-strewn streets.

We watched eyes following speeding-by vehicles, like ours.

I remember looking at Mike, as the kids stared in silence out the shuttle's rear windows, and whispering how I was praying that God would use this imagery to move Chase and Mia's hearts. There would certainly be a contrast between what we were seeing on that drive versus our resort.

Even when I reflected on what I had experienced in my own life, from my childhood days of living in a relatively low-income area of town to my not-so-nice college apartments to our now country home, I can see that I've lived a storybook life compared to these people.

The word "contrast" doesn't even begin to describe it.

C.S. Lewis said, "It is when we notice the dirt that God is most present to us: it is the very sign of His presence."[2]

I am definitely noticing the dirt today.

The dirt of my often taking for granted all the blessings that God provides every day. The dirt of regret for not responding graciously in every situation. The dirt of being judgmental towards others, as I now find myself asking God's forgiveness for originally responding to Mia's peanut butter request and home-sickness as ingratitude. For even now at the tender age of 9 years old, that precious girl is more compassionate and spiritual then I could ever hope to be.

So what does all this mean?

How do I respond over the next six days to this vacation in the midst of my curious mix of emotions? It feels like a rollercoaster of PRAISE BE TO GOD for this amazing once-in-a-life-time vacation to PROFOUND GUILT as my heart feels weighed down by the reality of this unfair world: the "have's" lounging on the sunny poolside and the "have not's" sweeping up the dead leaves floating on top.

How do I move forward without hurting my hardworking husband's feelings?

Yes, we are paying a fraction of the cost that this vacation is worth. But our time here still represents weeks of Mike's blood, sweat and tears. I definitely don't ever want to take for granted my husband's loving and steadfast commitment to diligently using his God-given gifts to financially support and encourage our family.

How do I set an example for my children by enjoying this vacation without condoning the excessive lifestyle... or leading them to believe that I don't care about those on the other side of the airport shuttle windows? I certainly don't want to dishonor the Lord, as surely all good comes from His hands.[3]

Lord, give me eyes to see...

~

Fast forward.

It's the final morning of our vacation, and we're about to say goodbye to "paradise."

Two bags of luggage, more pumped up than ever due to a steady diet of souvenirs, stand upright by our private villa's grand doors; these sturdy fellows appear to be screaming "TEN-HUT!" anxiously awaiting their departure to the boot camp of the airport baggage carousels.

Our Bermuda shorts and flimsy flip-flops have been pushed aside by Levi® jeans and Sorel® boots. In a mere 5 hours and two flights, the temperature will transition from a sunny tropical 80+ degrees to a Midwest Winter Weather alert of -2.

Sporting sun-kissed cheeks slathered with 100% aloe vera, two exhausted kids are slouched on the couch, plugged into ear buds, content to simply listen to their favorite iTunes® music. The usual end-of-vacation pleas for a final splash in the pool, inconveniently requested just a mere hour or less prior to our checkout, are noticeably absent. Don't get me wrong: the Huether's remain extremely grateful for this vacation that God has given us. But any illusion of perfection has been peeled back to reveal that there is really no such thing as paradise.

At least not here on Earth.

Yes, we witnessed poverty, for one. Outside the resort, people all around us are living in unacceptable conditions. But inside the walls, evidence of an imperfect world even in this seemingly beautiful place was gradually exposed...

"What's that rancid smell?" A stench from behind the dishwasher, which was discovered on the final day of our visit, turned out to be an infestation of mice between the appliance and the wall. Two days earlier, we noticed that the condo was occupied by more than the Huether clan; Mike witnessed a rat loafing in our sandals. I'm trying not to think of how this varmint was wandering around every night until it met its demise on the last night of our stay, courtesy of two resort employees armed with a broom.

Is something crawling on me? After the first day in our private pool, we were welcomed by a tiny army of resort residents that reveled in creeping up the patio lounge chairs. These red ants insisted that no human being would enjoy more than 10 minutes of uninterrupted bliss.

Will we have to pay for this? A mosaic tile peeling from a pool wall incited a cold slap of fear that we might be held responsible for the damage (and perhaps detained by one of the hundreds of faceless, black ski-masked Mexican police constantly patrolling the city's streets in their armored vehicles). However, upon careful examination, the area of tile departure was clearly patched well before our visit. (Anyway, that's what we're going with!) Still, the cost of its potential repair splashed the Huether CFO's brain (that's me) with every dive.

Gulp. We half-chuckled and half-cried at the bar patron who insisted on "swimming" in the center of one of the resort pools with what appeared to be the largest container of alcohol known to mankind. With that being said, the Huether family also was not immune to one of the 7 deadly sins; our dinner plates were piled high every morning for a gluttony fest, i.e. all-you-can-eat buffet, gorging ourselves with more food than our stomachs could or should handle.

Where's my tip? Although the resort staff was hospitable, every service was not only excessively priced but also inevitably followed by an extended hand – driven by either greed or the desperation of underpaid workers. In either case, by the end of the week, I grew weary and increasingly saddened by an attitude of self-entitlement, not only from the resort staff but also the guests (no doubt, the Huether's could be included in that category at one time or another).

Oh, yeah.

And then there was the drug lord who was busted three days before our arrival in a building right down the street from an area that we toured earlier during our stay.

Again, please don't misunderstand my straight-forwardness with discontent! Our family experienced the vacation of a lifetime, filled with amazing adventures in a new culture. We were also blessed with an abundant dose of bonding and much-needed Spring break from school and work. So I guess we did experience somewhat a taste of paradise, in that sense.

Lesson learned?

I don't believe that God is calling us to super-size our church tithe and other charitable contributions. (However, it's definitely a good idea to constantly pray and re-evaluate how to faithfully steward all that He's given us.) We likely will not give away all our belongings and become missionarys aboard. Or wallow in guilt over the life that God has given us.

He has placed me where I am for a reason.

Perhaps the lesson is not focused on a specific action but, rather, a reminder to never forget that the best is yet to come. No matter how good it may appear at times, nothing even comes close to the REAL PARADISE that God has prepared for His children after we leave this Earth.[4]

No rats. No self-indulgence. No guilt. No greed.

Just unity and justice for all who believe, richly living together in harmony not under some human ruler who values clothes, money and power. But under one perfect King Jesus, clothed in righteousness and equally loving everyone.

It's a God thing.

No frequent flyer miles needed.

---

1. For the Lord God is our sun and our shield. He gives us grace and glory. The Lord will withhold no good thing from those who do what is right. Psalm 84:11 (NLT)
2. *Yours, Jack: Spiritual Direction from C.S. Lewis* by C.S. Lewis
3. Every good and perfect gift is from above, coming down from the Father of the heavenly lights, who does not change like shifting shadows. James 1:17 (NLT)
4. Since you have been raised to new life with Christ, set your sights on the realities of heaven, where Christ sits in the place of honor at God's right hand. Think about the things of heaven, not the things of earth. For you died to this life, and your real life is hidden with Christ in God. And when Christ, who is your life, is revealed to the whole world, you will share in all his glory. Colossians 3:1-4 (NLT)

REST IN GEESE

Farewell, Perfectionist

I t's 2:15PM on Monday.

I've only crossed two items off my To-Do List. I have yet to shower, brush my teeth or eat lunch.

And I couldn't care less.

That's because the Lord gave me an incredible gift today. Two gifts, really. And I am filled with unspeakable joy.

I don't want this euphoria to end.

≈

L ast night, while drawing the curtains close in our kitchen, I glanced out the window at the 10+ acre pond about 1/2 mile beyond our front porch. I noticed that the water was inundated with white lumps.

"Hey, check this out, guys…"

One by one, Huether family members passed around the binoculars… and found their eyes instantly sprung open to twice their original size… oohing and awing over what appeared to be the world's largest cup of hot cocoa overloaded with puffy marshmallows under the nearly-set sun.

What was going on here?

My one remaining 50+ year-old brain cell started to kick in. Together with my husband Mike, we vaguely began to recall something that the previous owner shared among many things during the closing of our house several months ago. She mentioned there was a species of bird that flocked to this particular pond during a certain time of the year. In order to get more clarity, with the little clues mustered up from a hazy recollection of a past conversation, we did what curious people do when faced with the unknown.

We googled.

We discovered these white lumps were migrating Canadian Snow Geese. Literally, not one drop of water on the pond was visible, as hundreds of birds had completely taken over and snuggled in for the night. Very cool, we all thought. We thanked the Lord – as we've done countless times – for moving us unexpectedly out to the country. Then headed to our respective bedrooms to wrap up our Sunday night.

End of story?

Not quite.

∼

F ly forward to earlier this morning.

As usual, our Monday began with a 25-minute drive to school through near total darkness at 7AM, with the exception of a few mesmerizing slits of fiery purple and pink sky through slender clouds: a brilliant precursor to our always spectacular country sunrises.

After I dropped off the kids, I decided to head right back home instead of the grocery store... thanks to my inability to get out of bed early, jump in the shower and – most importantly – brush my teeth. If I had proceeded with my Monday shopping routine, the cashier at Walmart® would have likely been driven to her knees pleading a sincere "HELP ME!"... followed by a frantic flip-on of her checkout station light to request an immediate 15-minute break, i.e. scary-looking lady with halitosis in Aisle 6. The situation clearly would not have made for a good witness opportunity for Jesus.

So there I was driving down County Road 14... when I saw a scene that – literally – made me stop my gravel-pelleted Honda Pilot® in its country tracks.

BIRDS.

Hundreds...

AND HUNDREDS!

No, I corrected myself, as I scanned the sky and looked to the cornfield on my left.

Thousands...

AND THOUSANDS!

Snow geese were both blanketing the ground in the fields all around, as well as soaring en masse overhead. I pulled the vehicle over in knee-jerk fashion. (Praise God that we live in the boondocks or this story might be focusing on a fender bender.) My heart felt like it could burst from my chest. Eyes extended out beyond their widest reach. Jaw-dropping gasp practically smashing the vehicle's dashboard.

I CAN'T BELIEVE THIS!!!!

Honestly, I don't know if I was screaming aloud or in my mind. My eyes stretched beyond their natural capacity, as I sat dumbfounded over the white vibrating spots dotted all over the cornfield. I rolled down the window to hear an ethereal sound that conveyed both pandemonium and beauty.

The snow geese seemed to be randomly yelling directional commands at each other, *"To the left... to the left, buddy... COME ON!"* attempting to coax the few stray rebels back inside their pyramid flight formation. At the same time, in the midst of organized chaos, their collective sound was strangely in sync – and sung out with a hyper-exuberance unlike anything that I'd ever heard before! These birds totally believed their destination was someplace special.

And definitely worth celebrating.

My thoughts wandered to the Old Testament, specifically the Songs of Ascent (Psalms 120-134), which I'd been reading lately. I wondered if this wildly harmonious scene could be akin to the Israelites' massive excitement, as they made the annual trek up to Jerusalem to attend three pilgrim festivals.

Ok, maybe that's stretch.

All I know is that God was personally inviting me in for some glorious fun. I couldn't help feeling overwhelmed with gratitude for God's timing. In His sovereignty, God enabled me to see this unforgettable picture of His majesty – just one day after our family's return from Mexico. (Our flight home was nearly delayed by a mysterious glitch: the airline officials – who spoke virtually no English – claimed only three of us had legit tickets... and one Huether must remain in the country. Throw in the machine-gun toting security dudes – and we had a bona-fide harrowing situation! Once again, God came through for us in another example of His endless grace... which makes me think of the last line in the Gospel of John.[1])

Back to the birds.

I debated whether to sit in the Pilot... or run with total abandon onto the field. But a thought crossed my mind: *Will these guys attack me?* Oh, I hate when Fear attempts to steal my joy! I began to wonder if I was unwittingly becoming the next star in a reality show based on Alfred Hitchcock's 1963 classic "The Birds."

I fumbled for the camera mode on my iPhone®, snapped a few photos, and told myself: *I've got to get closer.* Settling back behind the steering wheel, I carefully reversed the car and turned around the opposite direction on the gravel road... as not to disturb my newfound feathered friends.

Too late.

The car's motion triggered what would be akin to an aerial stadium wave, as this wonderfully foul mob swooped and swirled in a movement of cascading white that no earthly words could capture in its exquisiteness. As they dived and spiraled and soared, this flock melodiously shouted out a one-of-a-kind collective "HURRAH!" that left me fumbling once again for more snapshots of the "National Geographic®" sort.

Darn.

They were too fast.

I missed it.

I abandoned my efforts to capture the imagery and headed as close to the birds as possible. I pulled to the side of the road... scooted over to the passenger's seat... rolled down the window... and began to salivate all over the car door. Never in my life had I seen such spectacular choreography.

A truck was approaching.

As it passed by, I looked at the elderly driver's face and saw a smile that relayed, *"Yah, it's pretty amazing, isn't it?"* along with one index finger lift from his steering wheel – the traditional sign of country camaraderie. He must have known that I was a first-timer to this classified local information.

I wonder what gave me away?

∼

Forty-five minutes later back at the ranch...

I've got to post this on Facebook®!

This thought in itself was extreme, as I have only posted a handful of times in the couple of years since I signed onto social media. However, a short video seemed to clearly be a give-God-the-glory moment that I wanted to ecstatically shout out to the world and invite everyone to see.

~

F our hours later...
No takers on the invite but lots of "Likes." Guess the no-shower-yet-today comment might have scared a few people away. Yah, my kids may be kinda frightened, too, when Mom shows up at school around 3:45PM in the exact same condition – and breath factor – as when she dropped them off.

So here I am, in the comfort of my Quiet Time spot. I have yet to eat lunch. And my chair has barely been warmed, as I keep jetting up and out of the synthetic leather and over to the window... still watching and mesmerized by a natural show of His out-of-this-world creation that continues on into the afternoon – despite the wind advisory and 30 mph gusts.

Boy, did God make those bird wings tough!

Even as I type right now, I am watching the umpteenth cluster of hundreds of Canadian snow geese swooping around, down and over the lake... seemingly suspended in air at some points along the way... always in a miraculous unity that boggles the mind and electrifies the heart.

I SO want to hug Jesus right now!

I mentioned two gifts, right?

The first is definitely the glimpse of His majesty.[2] That's the tangible gift that will be forever seared in my memory (and the 1G of photos my iPhone camera roll). But the second is equally extraordinary although not blatantly seen...

This just isn't me.

That's what I keep joyfully reminding myself, as I remember the woman who – not so long ago – was so imprisoned by her regimented schedule that she was unable to take the time to plant a garden. Write her first book. Or get to know Jesus intimately. (And I'm not talking "Bible study" here. I never really understood, until recently, how Quiet Time was so different – and so very critical for divine-human relationship.)

Basically, I was that "good Christian woman" who was drowning in her inability to say "no" and – instead – committed herself to WAY TOO MANY activities, including over-volunteering at church and school to not allowing her kids to take on greater responsibility, e.g. *"Oh, I'll just do it..."*

So the Lord began to rescue me.

When we first moved out to the country, I wasn't sure what to expect. It required a major shift in priorities. I guess my own migration of sorts... from insecurity and people-pleasing to complete surrender to *God's plan* for me. I had to release old fears of being alone. Isolated. Say goodbye to few relationships. Let go of some responsibilities that weren't the Lord's calling.

All these "things" were my own doing.

And they were doing me in.

So here I am, surprised and delighted, not only by the scene outdoors... but also the one inside my home.

A spectacular sight, indeed.

The dishes from last night still soaking in the sink. *EGADS!* Clumps of dog hair tumbling across the hardwood floor. Two loads of dirty laundry to boot! Now, I'm not saying that I've forever chucked all chores and running wild. I'm simply recognizing that sometimes life should be about so much more – that "more" being not only quality time with Jesus, but also loved ones like my two kiddos (who will be walking out the door into adulthood before too long).

Right now, I'm so appreciating that the Lord gave me a hubby who will understand today's God-ordained sidetrack from my domestic duties.[3] But mostly, I thank Jesus for freeing me from being an overachieving perfectionist – driven by a performance-based mindset that was, quite frankly, killing me. Or at least sucking most of the joy out of my life. Worse of all, I was robbing myself of experiencing the greatest Love of my life – and the heavenly bliss of becoming more like Him.

So goodbye, you tired old task-mastering lady.

And good riddance.

Like the snow geese, I'm headed to a better place.

A better me.[4]

Walking hand-in-hand with Jesus.

Making my own ascent into divine relationship, whether that means between me and Jesus or the peeps in my life.

Definitely worth celebrating!

I will, however, continue to brush my teeth and shower.

Starting tomorrow.

---

1. Jesus also did many other things. If they were all written down, I suppose the whole world could not contain the books that would be written. John 21:25 (NLT)
2. The heavens proclaim the glory of God. The skies display his craftsmanship. Day after day they continue to speak; night after night they make him known. They speak without a sound or word; their voice is never heard. Yet their message has gone throughout the earth, and their words to all the world. Psalm 19:1-4 (NLT)
3. Husbands, go all out in your love for your wives, exactly as Christ did for the church—a love marked by giving, not getting. Christ's love makes the church whole. His words evoke her beauty. Everything he does and says is designed to bring the best out of her, dressing her in dazzling white silk, radiant with holiness. And that is how husbands ought to love their wives. They're really doing themselves a favor—since they're already "one" in marriage. Ephesians 5:25-28 (MSG)
4. This means that anyone who belongs to Christ has become a new person. The old life is gone; a new life has begun! 2 Corinthians 5:17 (NLT)

MOVIE NIGHT

Good Grief

On a school night?

That was verbal jab #1 uttered as a response to my husband Mike following dinner.

I had my own vision of how this Sunday evening, the final one of the kids' Spring Break, would play out for our family. My expectations were that Mike and I would tuck the kids in right after dinner. That way, both young and old could hit the sack early... and be ready for a fresh start on Monday morning. I would take my 9-year-old Mia upstairs after her shower, and Mike would find a father-and-son kind of bonding activity – like shooting pool, playing cards, enjoying a board game, etc. – to ease Chase upstairs and into la-la land.

Apparently, Mike had his own plans.

Unfortunately, there was none of the usual "let's strategize about this evening" between Mom and Dad. Mike didn't communicate his intentions to me before sharing them with our 13-year-old son, who just happened to be in the room nearby – obviously listening to a behind the scenes play-by-play between the two of us. It looked like Mom would become the "bad guy" once again.

I just can't win.

Another movie?

Thankfully, verbal jab #2 was uttered in my mind rather than overflowing from an embittered heart. If spilled out from my lips, the negative tone in just those two words could have resulted in a one-two punch to knock out the entire evening – and then some! Oh, how I am forever indebted to God's Word, which has kept me from many a regretful comment spoken in haste only to leave a tear in the fabric of my most precious relationships. Thank you, Proverbs 21:23[1], Ephesians 4:29[2], James 1:26[3], Psalm 141:3[4] and others too numerous to mention!

An uncomfortable silence seemed to painfully linger between Mike and me. The previously just-a-nudge of annoyance had now morphed into an all-out assault on my weary emotional state, i.e. *I love you people, BUT MAMA NEEDS TO RETURN TO "NORMAL!"*

My practical side (which I really do despise) screamed that freedom, i.e. Spring Break, must come to an end. Bills must be paid. Projects tackled. Bathrooms cleaned. I sensed the very real danger of a disgruntled (ok, maybe hostile is a more accurate depiction) homemaker about to become unleashed. Anger seemed on the verge of seething out from every inch of my "Mom-relaxed-too-much-and-will-pay-tomorrow" body.

At this point, there seemed no way out. If Mike reneged on what seemed to already be a promise to Chase, I would have two angry men on my hands. One dejected husband who undoubtedly would feel lessened of his masculinity and authority from a dictating wife. One rejected son who would resent his mother for – once again – putting the kibosh on a glorious night of brain-numbing TV viewing.

What's a mama to do?

In my mind, I was only trying to do the right thing: Get the people into bed at a reasonable time, so that the week ahead would be off to the best possible start.

But at that moment, I felt resentment overtaking me. If not for the Holy Spirit – literally – keeping my mouth closed, the night would have been nothing short of disastrous on so many levels – and in so many relationships.[5]

I avoided eye contact with Mike. Silently huffed into the laundry room. Quickly stuffed the washer with a load of towels and jeans, so Chase would have a clean pair in the morning. Shouted out a couple of commands to the boys about transferring the clothes to the dryer when the washer was done.

Then I took Mia upstairs to move forward with MY plan for the evening.

~

Mia and I had a wonderful tuck-in filled with the routine tickle, an enlightening reading of Proverbs 23, and some great conversation about life. I forgot about the mental wrestling related to the Huether boys and just enjoyed my time with Mia. Cozied up in bed with my precious little girl, I accidentally drifted off to sleep with that sweet "Mia" smell and softness resting on my shoulder.

One-and-a-half hours later, I abruptly woke up drenched in sweat – the inevitable consequences of a double body heat overload in a twin-size bed. I snuck out Mia's bedroom door and down the stairs to see the movie's closing credits scrolling over the TV screen in our living room. Even after a reading of Proverbs with Mia just a short while earlier, the ugliness of resentment returned with a nasty full mental assault.

I was not resisting.

Ever have those times when you KNOW that you're not acting right... but for some bizarre reason, YOU JUST KEEP

DOING IT?! This was the mindset – or should I say emotional prison – where I was stuck at that moment.

It wasn't pretty.

I said goodnight to Chase, got ready for bed, and slipped under the sheets... praying that I would fall asleep quickly to avoid any interaction with my hubby while in this destructive mental condition. While alone in bed, I prayed.

And prayed.

And PRAYED.

Lord, please help. I know these thoughts aren't right. But I just can't stop them!

I felt Mike slide into bed. I turned away from his side of the mattress and – with my eyes squinted open – could see the glow of his cell phone faintly illuminating the room. It seemed like one of those "I can't keep my eyes off it" swaying double lights that crisscross the sky when you're driving around on a Saturday night... and your kids beg you "Can we track it down?" You say "ok" and spend 30 minutes locating its originating source... only to discover that it's simply a devious trick to lead you to some retail outlet that you can't afford to visit but now your kiddos really want to stop inside and make a random purchase.

AAAYYYHHH!!!

Do I seem irritated?

Every night, Mike routinely checks his cell phone in bed before turning off the lights. I rarely ask what he's doing. But this night, after what seemed like FOREVER of that cell phone light blaring through my shut eyelids, I offered up these words slathered in testiness:

What are you DOING?! That light is SO BRIGHT!

Those were not exclamations of joy.

But oh, that sweet man.

Mike gently commented something about checking out the scores. (I say "something about" because, when I get that irritated, I cannot listen and rarely remember a word that is said.) Then he shut off his phone.

I mean, SERIOUSLY! (That is, incredulously.)

How many commandments can I break in one evening?!

As I drifted off to sleep, Ephesians 4:26 lingered in my head...

"Don't sin by letting anger control you. Don't let the sun go down while you are still angry..."

~

Next thing I know, my alarm clock was ringing. It was 4:45AM. I had overslept again. But it wasn't the clock's fault, as I'd pressed "snooze" at least a dozen times over the past 45 minutes. During those brief times of intermittent consciousness, I'd been praying to God... pleading for Him to alter my thinking.

And change my heart.

I started to rattle off the attributes of God in A-B-C format. You know, one attribute for every letter of the alphabet. Then I offered up thanksgiving for my family. Next, I replayed the amazing, relationship-bonding, God-honoring past seven days that we enjoyed together. Suddenly, I felt His Light burst through my prayers of forgiveness and praise in the form of an "Ah-a" moment...

"... for anger gives a foothold to the devil."

Merriam-Webster describes "foothold" as a place from which an advance (as in military operations) is made. The Bible makes it clear that spiritual warfare is taking place all around us; this reality exists whether or not we choose to believe it.[6]

Basically?

The Enemy of my soul was attacking me.

And I fell for it.

I had not been irritated like last night for a very long time. Over the past few months and days, Jesus has been dramatically transforming our family.

And the Father of Lies would do anything to stop it.

Have you ever felt trapped in a *mental onslaught* of discontent and negativity? Isn't that where the destruction of relationships begins? I've read that the deadliest of the 10 commandments is the last one listed in Exodus 20:17, i.e. Do not covet. Coveting basically amounts to flat-out selfishness. Your wants become gotta-haves that trump everyone, including your fellow man and God Almighty. Of course, that's no good! But it's also *down-right dangerous,* because this temptation takes place in your mind. If left to simmer, these no-good thoughts boil over into *action* – leaving a devastating scar on a loved one's heart, while you're tortured with regret and guilt, i.e. *why-on-Earth-did-I-do-that?!*[7]

Here's another nasty catch, which may be the most sinister of all: Often the actions causing the most destruction aren't the biggies but the subtle ones, especially if layered over time.

Like the evil eye.

A harsh voice tone.

One or two choice words.

Yikes.

All of a sudden, the Lord takes me on a mental journey back through the 25+ years that I've been married to Mike. It's almost as though Jesus opened up the "Chris Huether" photo album, focusing on glimpses of my marriage long passed by...

God brought Mike into my life during college, when I was suffering from an eating disorder. When he discovered my problem, Mike never condemned me. He not only married me, but also provided encouragement to help see me through to victory after an eight-year battle that could have killed me.[8] Even to this day, Mike has never said anything but complimentary things about my body. Literally, he thanks God *every morning* – aloud for both me and the Lord to hear – how I am the woman of his dreams and more sexy to him than ever at 50+ years. (Sounds pretty crazy, doesn't it?) Mike's unconditional love – regardless of what I look like – helps me focus on what's really important, which is growing more like Christ on the inside.

I then recall a turning point in our marriage, less than 10 years ago. In our living room by the fireplace, I shared the "there's-got-to-be-something-more-than-this" speech. Up to this point, I had only seen Mike cry three times – this day being one of them. We'd recently started attending a local church, which was launching a read-the-Bible-in-a-year initiative. We agreed to give it a try. Little did we know that the next couple years would bring some of the toughest times of our married life, including a job loss and relocation. Our commitment to turn to God's word *together* brought us hope and strength, not only individually but as a couple. Ultimately, God intended that "living room talk" to serve as a springboard to our eternal salvation – less than one year after we started reading the Bible daily.

I'm in awe that the Creator of the Universe would so thoughtfully handpick the perfect husband for me – especially when the two of us disgraced Him during the first 40+ years of our lives. Even more amazing? Jesus was walking beside with me all that time – even when I stubbornly refused to acknowledge Him. Today, my marriage is stronger than I could have ever imagined! I'm falling more in love with my husband – *and Jesus* – every day. Why? It's all because of God's grace and His ongoing desire to help me see the Truth vs. the lies.

What is the Truth?

Mike is a Godly man who reads Scripture daily. His life is a testimony to what it's like to work with integrity. Mike is my best friend who helped save me from killing myself with the illusion that I can or should be perfect. Mike encourages me to be who God created me to be, even allowing days to go by without dinner on the table – so I can put my thoughts on paper or serve in women's Bible study.

Mike is a praying man who never misses a morning of laying in bed with his wife, lifting up praises and petitions to the Lord for every member of our family, as well as co-workers, school-mates and relatives who – sadly – have yet to know the rock-solid love and beyond-amazing adventure of following Jesus.

Mike is a loving father who hangs out with his kids on the weekends, often pushing aside office duties or home mainte-nance activities. In other words, Mike knows how to prioritize... and sometimes that means that the grass grows knee-high before mowing or a door handle remains loose for just a little while longer.

Oh, don't get me wrong.

Mike does have his flaws.

But when I start to think about my shortcomings – I mean, not once has Mike complained when dinner consists of Lipton® Extra Noodle Soup and homemade nachos with few bruised grapes on the side – the proverbial light bulb starts to glow.

The problem last night wasn't Mike.

It was me.

This revelation comes nearly 12 hours after the initial words that sparked the resentment flame. Even when I gave up and went down a bad mental path, my loving God never gave up on me. Thanks to His never-ending grace plus the "Ah-ha" illumi-nation courtesy of the Holy Spirit, I'm experiencing the good grief needed for the Lord to cleanse me from my sin.

The sin of ingratitude.

Thank you, Jesus.

I asked for forgiveness. Celebrated His righteousness. And thanked God that He has made these incidents of pity parties, grumbling and mama-out-of-control so much more few-and-far-between that I could have ever hoped possible.

It's progress not perfection, Sisters.

Best of all?

I feel no condemnation. No sending Chris to the "dark room" of shame and guilt, which was the place that defined me during my legalism days. (Legalism meaning that I was unwittingly living out my spirituality as a rule-follower vs. Jesus-lover.) Rather, it's the peace-filled freedom of knowing that I don't need to be perfect. Just perfectly in love with the One who saved me not only on the day that I said "yes" to His free gift of eternal salvation, but this morning when I was wandering in darkness.

The darkness of a life without Jesus.[9]

Now I can't wait to say I'm sorry and hug my hubby when he walks in the door before "dinner" tonight. (Notice how that was strategically placed in parentheses. I may need to offer up some apologies for my transgressions in today's family food preparation, too.) And belt out "Amazing Grace" on the 3:45PM drive from school with my children.

Hmmm... maybe there will be a little damage there.

To the eardrums, that is.

Ahhh, more grief.

But at least there's some good in there.

Maybe?

---

1. Watch your tongue and keep your mouth shut, and you will stay out of trouble. Proverbs 21:23 (NLT)
2. Don't use foul or abusive language. Let everything you say be good and helpful, so that your words will be an encouragement to those who hear them. Ephesians 4:29 (NLT)
3. If you claim to be religious but don't control your tongue, you are fooling yourself, and your religion is worthless. James 1:26 (NLT)
4. Take control of what I say, O Lord, and guard my lips. Psalm 141:3 (NLT)

5. A wise woman builds her home, but a foolish woman tears it down with her own hands. Proverbs 14:1 (NLT)

6. Satan, who is the god of this world, has blinded the minds of those who don't believe. They are unable to see the glorious light of the Good News. They don't understand this message about the glory of Christ, who is the exact likeness of God. 2 Corinthians 4:4 (NLT)

7. Temptation comes from our own desires, which entice us and drag us away. These desires give birth to sinful actions. And when sin is allowed to grow, it gives birth to death. James 1:14-15 (NLT)

8. Suffering from bulimia or another eating disorder? Please read the following link and seek professional help. It's not too late! https://www. webmd.com/mental-health/eating-disorders/bulimia-nervosa/bulimia-effects-body#1

9. How foolish can you be? After starting your new lives in the Spirit, why are you now trying to become perfect by your own human effort? Have you experienced so much for nothing? Surely it was not in vain, was it? I ask you again, does God give you the Holy Spirit and work miracles among you because you obey the law? Of course not! It is because you believe the message you heard about Christ. Galatians 3:3-5 (NLT)

DIVING DEEP

Uke and Lele

I'm sitting here staring at a fish.

And lovin' every minute of it. That's what God's Word has done to me.

~

Oh, no. Where is Uke?

I looked in the fish bowl, and Uke was nowhere to be found.

Uke is my daughter Mia's lone GloFish®, one of two that was purchased about five months ago with Christmas gift money. His purple companion was the now-deceased Lele. Yes, they actually do glow when placed under LED lights. No, these fish aren't musically inclined. Uke and Lele were named after Mia's musical instrument of choice, i.e. the ukulele.

Just a little clarification there.

Now back to the dearly departed.

We suspect that Lele was infectious from day #1, because my husband Mike was cleaning scum from the bowl weekly – since the day that she was scooped up and plopped inside the plastic sandwich-size bag from a local store's aquatic section. No longer sucking up bacteria, Uke has not seemed too upset that Lele departed to the big aquarium in the sky. Not only does the fishbowl stay clean, but Uke was clearly more at peace.

He was no longer banging his head against the glass.

Halleluiah.

Let me describe the scene: the fish bowl is an approximately 3-gallon glass container (economically purchased at Walmart in the Household Essentials department for $6.99). It rests on the upper shelf of a defunct computer armoire, which now houses all the stuff that my kids refuse to stow away in their mudroom cubbies. In other words, it's the dumping ground for any straggling pieces of paper, library books and whatnot.

Kind of like a junk drawer.

Just 1,000 times the size.

On the upper shelf, Uke resides solo in a penthouse of sorts. He shares the space with adjacent box of Kleenex®. From time to time, our lovable I'll-consume-anything-including-broccoli 1½-year-old Siberian Husky, Redd, successfully rips down and destructively shreds the box, strewing pieces all over the first floor of our home. Despite these occasional tissue paper kidnappings, Uke seemed relatively safe in his lofty habitat.

Besides the fact that, right now, he's nowhere to be found. And his living quarters are less than 1/2 the size of a very petite powder room sink.

I'm thankful no one captured my search for Uke on film. As if he was outfitted with feet rather than fins, I scanned not only the inside of the bowl... but around the exterior... even opening up the cabinet doors below. *I mean, how difficult could it be? Why can't I see him?* In the aquatic world, Uke was a standout dude, brightly colored with shades of gold and striped with orange.

The two youthful members of the Huether search party had already given up: my son Chase was downing his Muscle Milk®;

his sister Mia was spreading butter on her breakfast toast. Apparently, they traded in their Jr. rescuer badges for hunger and the greater need to start the school day in a timely manner.

We needed to be in the car in less than ½ hour.

Mom, perhaps this is not the best time to search for a fish? said one of my two marine life defectors.

Those words of compassion from my got-to-get-there-early 7th grader seemed to be the trigger that sparked movement in our golden-fin boy. I glimpsed a pair of huffing gills camouflaged inside the fluorescent bushes of the plastic island on the center floor of the glass jar.

He had fallen prey to the temptation of exploring an underwater forbidden zone.

And now he was gasping for life.

I removed Uke's hefty homestead from the shelf. Then I gently placed the 40-pound jar centerstage on our kitchen island, so as not to create more havoc for the fish – and my marriage – by cracking the granite surface in this mildly reckless venture. From the start, my hubby wasn't too keen on taking on these two chums. However, they were Christmas presents, which served as a trump card of sorts. I also threw in the kid-will-reap-responsibility spiel. This duo-whammy of "Please can we buy them?" on the Daddy man worked in achieving the thumbs-up to welcome two new members to the Huether clan.

But at the present moment?

I'm kind of regretting that Mike took the bait.

Next, I proceeded to move forward with what I believed to be a Biblically-correct attempt to resolve this sticky situation: Gather many advisors to contemplate the wisest strategy for this fish's freedom. A little Proverbs 15:22 in action was on the mind of this here's-an-opportunity-to-train-them-up" mamma:

Plans go wrong for lack of advice; many advisers bring success.

I threw out the question of the day:
What should we do, gang?
More "compassion" was promptly dispersed by big bro.
Mom, perhaps this is not the best time to save a fish?
Hmm.

Not quite the response that I desired in this seize-the-teachable-moment.

I turned to Mia and presented her with two options. As the person who welcomed Uke into our family, my animal-loving nine-year-old is really the only one who could ultimately decide Uke's fate. The final decision, which was certain to be one of life vs. death, needed to be suited to her comfort level.

The first option? Allow Uke to dislodge himself. I mean, after all, he got himself into this predicament. Perhaps he could also wriggle himself out. Then I rushed out of the kitchen for a few moments... and returned with a visual aid to assist in my presentation of the second option. (As you may have already surmised, I intended the props to subtly emphasize that this upcoming option was Mom's preferred one.)

The second option? Mom could slip on some plastic gloves. (I liked our finned friend. But there was NO WAY that I was dipping my bare skin into those cloudy waters infested with mysterious floaties.) I would then carefully reach down and delicately separate the branches. That way, Uke could – hopefully – swim out from their clutches unscathed. Essentially, my hands would become a human rendition of the Jaws of Life® minus the hydraulics and circular saw.

I cautioned Mia that both options posed some risk. Each one could result in either life.

Or death.

My heart was beating. I was mentally preparing myself to dive in. And then Mia selected the option that I least expected.

Let's leave him alone until we get home from school later today.

Hmm.

Yes, I offered a choice.

But I really didn't think Mia would choose THAT one!

I hate when that happens.

We left Uke, gasping in his misery, and headed off to school.

~

Two hours later, I was back at the home front.

The kids were now undoubtedly immersed in their schoolwork, while Uke's dire straits were far from their think tanks. Mom, on the other hand, had walked by the glass death chamber several times since returning home.

I couldn't take it anymore.

There was no way I could sit all day watching this poor guy sucking in and out his final breaths. I slipped on the blue latex gloves. Looked closely at the bowl, diagnosing the situation like a surgeon. Then eased my hands into that watery graveyard, personally entering into Uke's self-created mess. After a few not-so-gentle shakes of that deadly foliage, Uke was finally set free.

Unfortunately, he spent a few minutes floating sideways.

It was not pretty.

I added a few cups of fresh water to fully revive him.

~

S o now I stare victoriously at the fish bowl – and pray that my husband never discovers what I really do during the day. I'm rescuing and meditating on fish – and actually going as far as to write about it – while our human habitat is in dire need of its own revival, e.g. vacuuming, dusting, etc.

Seriously, though, this seemingly minor incident has broadened my perspective of God's loving kindness. How often has He reached down when I'm stuck in sin? When I drift away from the safety of His perfect ways and into the dark clutches of believing *my way* is better? Often, I'm fully aware that "I shouldn't even go there." Yet time and time again, He mercifully plunges in... lifts me up from my self-made mess – always in perfect timing – so I can swim again in His glorious presence.

It's a never-gonna-let-you-go-grip.

With no slap on the dorsal.

I'm talking about that no condemnation thing.[1]

When I first started to read the Bible, I remember thinking: *When will all this stuff make sense? When will I become so in tune to God... that I will see Him all around me and every day?*

In one of my first Bible studies, the leader encouraged us newbies to look for God in the small stuff. For example, when driving through green lights, she reflects on how God's laws create a perfect community united in love.[2] I mean, just imagine a city with no traffic laws! Each person would determine his or her own speed limit, when to stop or go, who has the right of way, etc. In a world of self-driven people, we're destined for a total crash and burn![3] This Godly gal also shared how everyday objects – from the bathroom mirror to her vacuum cleaner – serve as visual prompts to pray for people or situations.[4]

Oh, I thought, how I want to live that way!

I tried and tried and tried.

But just minutes or hours after my morning Bible reading, I

zoned out into the logistics of life. At the end of my day, I would mentally beat myself up asking:

What happened?!

Why can't I hang out with Jesus all day?

Yet I continued to get up early every morning to read God's Word, regardless of whether or not I walked away afterwards "feeling" anything or wandered away by mid-day. I persevered because, deep down inside, I was drawn to the possibility that there was a greater power – *and a deeper love* – somewhere in *His glorious Kingdom* that had to be better than my feeble "It's all about me" world.

Finally, I'm starting to not only see it, but *feel* it.

Or should I say see and feel *Him*.

This morning, my prayer for greater spiritual insight was answered in a wonderfully *other-than* way, which is so characteristic of my Father God. All He does for His children, like me, is so special. So intimate. So uniquely designed to an individual's needs. Yet He loves each one of us equally. God shows no favoritism, which eliminates any temptation to compare or compete with others. (That means God loves me just as much as any of his original disciples or C.S. Lewis or any notables in the Christian faith. Go figure!)[5]

Today, the Lord revealed His glory to me personally in the rescue of one of His most fragile creations – a tiny fish that could literally fit in the palm of my hand. In doing so, He reminded me to celebrate His mercy. Revel in His sovereignty. And stand in awe of His Almighty hand that reached down, in the person of Jesus Christ, to rescue little me from the clutches of sin and – ultimately – physical and spiritual death. Every day, I'm swimming in His amazing grace... as He freed me from Satan's lies that left me feeling stuck, like a small fish in the big sea, heading nowhere with no meaning or purpose in life.

So now I'm praying, Lord, bring on the fish tales! Show me

how to drive through traffic lights with my hands extended out the window in praise (preferably with my eyes open, thank you). Awaken me to the spiritual side of every aspect of this life, from my living room rug to our lawn mover.

I'm diving in deep.

Because when I start to see God in even the smallest details and moments of daily life, He reveals to me more of His majesty.

Even in a fish bowl.

Do I hear an Amen?

Or how about a splash of Hallelujah.

---

1. So now there is no condemnation for those who belong to Christ Jesus. And because you belong to him, the power of the life-giving Spirit has freed you from the power of sin that leads to death. The law of Moses was unable to save us because of the weakness of our sinful nature. So God did what the law could not do. He sent his own Son in a body like the bodies we sinners have. And in that body God declared an end to sin's control over us by giving his Son as a sacrifice for our sins. He did this so that the just requirement of the law would be fully satisfied for us, who no longer follow our sinful nature but instead follow the Spirit. Romans 8:1-4 (NLT)

2. God has now revealed to us his mysterious will regarding Christ—which is to fulfill his own good plan. And this is the plan: At the right time he will bring everything together under the authority of Christ—everything in heaven and on earth. Ephesians 1:9-10 (NLT)

3. Jesus said, "Don't misunderstand why I have come. I did not come to abolish the law of Moses or the writings of the prophets. No, I came to accomplish their purpose. I tell you the truth, until heaven and earth disappear, not even the smallest detail of God's law will disappear until its purpose is achieved. So if you ignore the least commandment and teach others to do the same, you will be called the least in the Kingdom of Heaven. But anyone who obeys God's laws and teaches them will be called great in the Kingdom of Heaven." Matthew 5:17-19 (NLT)

4. Never stop praying. Be thankful in all circumstances, for this is God's will for you who belong to Christ Jesus. 1 Thessalonians 5:17-18 (NLT)

5. For the Lord your God is the God of gods and Lord of lords. He is the great God, the mighty and awesome God, who shows no partiality and cannot be bribed. Deuteronomy 10:17 (NLT)

THE DREAM

Crazy in a God Way

H*ow's country living?*
        It definitely could have been my imagination, but the woman's words with tilted smile seemed ever-so-slightly tinged with sarcasm. She was a co-leader in a Bible study that I joyfully participated in for years, that is, before the Lord moved our family 20 miles outside city limits.

Almost a year ago, the Lord rocked my world. He took me completely by surprise. Redefined what I considered "normal." And transformed me, inside and out. With just one decision, He changed my everything.

My activities.

My priorities.

My perspective.

My relationships, especially with Jesus.

I can't thank Him enough.

∾

My husband Mike and I like people. We also like pizza delivery. Living in the boondocks away from the civilized world (and convenient food) was not something that ever felt like a burning desire. It was only about a year prior to our move that we started to toy with the idea of looking for an acreage outside city limits.

What triggered thoughts of a potential relocation? Our family has moved numerous times before, but really never by choice; my hubby works in the volatile industry of animal health and veterinary medicine. I attribute the initial spark to one of the pastors at a local Bible-based church that our family was attending at the time. He was teaching on the joy of the Lord and asked a question something to this effect: *What is one thing that brings you joy that isn't now part of your life... maybe it seems impossible, but perhaps God is just waiting to bless you with?*

A couple of hours after the sermon, while eating lunch overlooking suburbia from our small dining room table, I asked Mike somewhat hesitantly with a slight chuckle, "Ok, Mike. What brings you joy?" My hesitancy stemmed from the fact that many a man, I believe, when asked that question by his wife, could head down a – should I say – risqué path. I wasn't quite sure that I wanted to know the answer! But, nevertheless, a sense of marital intrigue overwhelmed me.

"Hunting," Mike replied matter-of-factly.

Huh?

I knew that my husband had been an avid hunter in his high school days. (Although arguably, many of those outings were conducted unscrupulously in the cornfields outside his hometown. At least that's what legend tells us. By legend, I mean those stories that make Mom gasp when Dad spontaneously shares them at the dinner table with the kiddos. They usually involve local law enforcement officials. Mike was, obviously, not a follower of Jesus in his teenage days.) Over the 25+ years that we've been married, Mike has enjoyed a handful or less trips to hunt with Uncle Tim back in Southwestern Nebraska. But he never mentioned hunting under the category of soul longings.

Apparently, the sermon had unearthed his primal man.

Hence, we began weekly "Homes" section searches in our local newspaper. Our mission? We hoped to discern whether this revelation, surprising unveiled from the pulpit, was a God thing. Every Sunday before leaving for church, we glanced through real estate listings. Only twice did we find properties that appeared worthy of uprooting our day-of-rest routine and high-tailing to the acreage scene. However, with those two houses, we realized the truth of "looks can be deceiving." Or more accurately, how looks can kill – kill the dream, that is!! It became clear that any photo could be strategically angled to provide a twisted picture of reality.

With the prospects looking particularly dreary, we didn't even get as far as signing on a realtor. We certainly did not feel even close to the point of calling our bank to see if we could qualify for a home loan.

Nevertheless, we continued to be intrigued by the notion of country life. Although I must confess, the thought of spending my time "in the boonies" for 8+ hours daily, while Mike was working and the kids schooling it, sent a chill down my wimpy "I can't imagine being totally out there alone!" spine.

After a little over a year passed by, Mike and I determined that it was not God's plan for our family. Apparently, it wasn't Jesus calling that morning when joy of the Lord was preached so passionately... and the pastor seemed to be speaking directly to Mike and me. We decided that it was time to stop our usual – and, at this point, quite depressing – Sunday morning routine of checking out the real estate listings.

Little did I know that just a few hours after calling it quits was precisely the day in which the Lord would soon be saying, "You're moving, Sweet Sister."

He was about to throw us the Master curve ball.

SUNDAY 5PM

Later that evening, Mike was preparing dinner as usual. (Oh, how the Lord blessed this kitchen-illiterate mamma with a hubby who loves to cook!) Lackadaisically, I asked my hubby, "Did you look at the 'Open Houses' this morning?" He replied no, and I slowly began flipping to the Real Estate section of the Lincoln Journal Star®. I couldn't help myself. Over the past 300+ days, it was my go-to Sunday reading routine.

My eyes widened.

My jaw dropped.

Yes, it was just one photo. But it looked pretty darn promising. The price for this too-good-to-be-true property – listed just a little over 24 hours ago – was less than our current mortgage. And it was nestled inside 20 acres just 25 minutes from Lincoln. I hurried to my computer, pulled up the full-blown listing with more than two dozen photos, and couldn't believe it was reality. This acreage was certainly worth more than the price listed!

But we had missed the "Open House" earlier in the day.

TUESDAY 5PM

Just two days later, our family was headed to "the house" with Andrea, a dear friend who is also a realtor. (Mike had attempted to drive by solo the night before, but found himself lost – in a torrential downpour, no less – in the middle of nowhere on a low maintenance road.) She was happy to check it out with us. Andrea, too, was curious about the discrepancy between the photos and the listing price. We traveled for what seemed like a long drive down the highway, over railroad tracks and across a few miles of gravel. At the sight of the "Rock Ends Here" sign, which seemed to be the official end of civilization as we know it (and possibly an encounter with Freddie or Jason in the flesh), I began mulling over in my mind the wisdom of this venture, i.e. *where are we and is this even legit?* A break in the trees revealed what undoubtedly over a dozen other families (according to the listing agent) also discovered in the three days since the house entered the market:

This was the real deal.

After waiting in line behind a tall dude donning a cowboy hat (and somewhat convincingly carrying the aura of a wealthy cattleman), Andrea led our family through the house, my dragging tongue leaving a definitive trail on the custom wood floors – that is, when I wasn't involuntarily spilling out exclamations that make your realtor cringe, i.e. "Don't give away that you like it or they'll jack up the price!"

"WOW!" "OH, MY!" "THAT IS SOOOO COOL!!"

You get the picture.

No house stage fright here.

As we exited the building, Mike and I looked at each other and almost simultaneously mouthed:

"We don't stand a chance of getting this property."

WEDNESDAY 7:30AM

Early the next day, Andrea sent me "the text." I place those two words in parentheses, because they marked not just a cliché turning point... but an all-out, about-face that would soon take our family onto a radically new path for each of our lives.

Yesterday, after Andrea showed the property to our family, we confessed to her – and each other – that what Mike and I were feeling transcended more than just an enthusiastic shout of "WE LOVE IT!" We couldn't even categorize the experience as a dream come true, because it was so far beyond any expectations of anything we could have ever imagined![1] Everything about the house seemed perfect for our family, from Mike's always-wished-I-had natural gas range to the distressed kitchen cabinets. (Distressed?! What a novel idea for a family with two Siberian Huskies plus a pair of we-love-pretend-play children whose creative ideas sometimes result in physical disaster, i.e. a dink in the wall or a scratch here and there.)

But apparently, others also saw their own potential miracle in the making with this heavenly acreage. The seller had received five offers, Andrea explained. She had no idea what those offers looked like in terms of dollar amount. Then she asked if we wanted to go for it.

Seriously?

Mike and I looked at each other with expressions that could only be construed as communicating one thing:

This is nuts.

But Something told us to give it a shot.

WEDNESDAY 1PM

Later that afternoon, Mike and I sat in a Lincoln coffee shop with Andrea, praying about a fair price to offer the seller.

I am a "Consumer Reports®" gal. In other words, I suck the life (and probably fun, if you ask my husband) out of every major purchase that our family makes. Spontaneous is simply not a word in the Chris Huether vocabulary. In fact, when I was working as a freelance copywriter, a client once told me that she loved working with me because I was anal in terms of my detail-oriented disposition.

Ouch.

So when we're talking about looking at a house ONCE and

making an offer LESS THAN 24 HOURS LATER, I remember thinking that either this is the Lord.

Or Mike and I have both lost our minds.

We could also lose our financial security (if there really is such a thing); an offer on this house meant that we could potentially have two mortgages.

No caution was thrown to this wind.

We were pressing on.

As insane as it all sounded.

Strangely enough, the insanity felt darn good. I kinda liked my chains of practicality being crushed. Obliviated is more like it. We could have two mortgage payments, while waiting on the sale of our existing house (which wasn't even on the market). Yet the experience was so freeing – so wildly exhilarating – SO NOT ME. This formerly meticulous girl was thoroughly enjoying ripping up her anal (oops, I mean annual) subscription to rigorous research and logical purchases.

I had no idea that being impractical was this much fun.

Thankfully, during this 12-hour freedom fest from the old Chris, Jesus affirmed that this seemingly world-will-think-we're-nuts adventure was, indeed, Him. He was sovereignly moving all the pieces of this relocation puzzle beautifully in place. In the short time from Andrea's morning text message to the three of us gathering for afternoon coffee....

JESUS qualified us for financial approval to place an offer on a new home, while still owning a second one. When I miraculously reached her at 8:05AM, the extremely busy mortgage lender at our bank confirmed that "it was a miracle" that she was available and able to work with us. She emailed the approval letter just one hour after my request.

JESUS miraculously cleared three people's schedules, i.e. me, Mike and Andrea, so we could not only meet at the coffee shop, but also still pick up our kiddos on-time at school later that day.

JESUS graciously enabled me to reach our insurance agent on that hectic morning to double-check for any unforeseen financial repercussions of moving out of Lincoln to a nearby small town of 500+ in a different county. (Ok, there was still a little practicality lingering in me, but it was Holy Spirit-led.) In the midst of all the chaos, I'm still in awe – and grateful – to God for providing me with the wisdom and time to inquire in advance about the possible changes to our homeowner's insurance.

By the way, it turned out that country living was cheaper.

Can you see a sovereign pattern, here?

Many more miracles happened that day. And every step of the way, I – literally – felt like Jesus was holding my hand... and gently leading me through each piece of – what would later be revealed after the move – His salvation plan for our family.

At the end of the day, Mike and I decided to offer the owner what we believed the property was worth versus the listing price. (Another God thing is that Andrea is married to a builder and, therefore, able to accurately list all the assets of the property.) The price that we offered was several thousand dollars over what the owner listed. Seemingly crazy, right? But righteousness was where the Lord was leading us.

Just three hours, doing the right thing proved victorious.

WEDNESDAY 4PM

Shortly after school, while shopping for flip-flops at the local mall with my daughter Mia, I was blessed with another life-transforming communication from Andrea.

This time, it was in the form of a phone call.

Congratulations. You got the house!

I – kid you not – fell to my knees, unabashedly weeping a wondrous trio of disbelief, fear and happiness, right there on the glossy tiles of Dillard's®. Mia was crying, too, but more so as a desperate plea to her looney mamma to stand the heck up... because I was subsequently drawing the attention of the entire shoe sales team. But hey!

That's one way to get prompt service, right?

Mia and I never found the perfect shoes. But as we exited the store's doors that afternoon, I realized that God did provide the perfect flip-flop.

He was turning my world upside down.

From city chaos to country peace.

Where I would learn what it's like to know real joy.

That is, the out-of-this-world love of Jesus.

$\sim$

A n entire book could not list all the miracles (and tests of faith, I will not lie) during the transition period of our old to new housing...

We muddled through 1½ months of nail-biting days waiting for our previous house to sell. (Interesting sidenote: The day after we made the offer on our new home, the loan officer called to say that a mistake was made; we actually could not afford two house mortgages! But she graciously took responsibility for the error and allowed us to move forward anyway with a bridge loan. Crazy-cool God thing? You gotta believe it, baby!)

We encountered an unexpected detour when one U-Haul® rental morphed into three – and I'm not just talking three trips.[2] THREE WEEKENDS. Hence, three billings. Over the course of our 25+ year marriage, our many prior relocations were new-hire-package deals provided by Mike's employers, so this move was our first solo effort. (In other words, we had no clue what we were doing!) Our new house was just outside the boundaries of most Lincoln movers' territories, so their answer was "no" to our inquiries for help.

I was temporarily lured into a dark pit of doubt when a horrifying article ran in our local newspaper the morning before all our belongings were officially moved. It was an anniversary feature about a deranged man who several years ago – yup, you guessed it – murdered a woman and her daughter at their home in the country, while the husband was out of town. Subsequently, Mike's work dictated that he travel to China the day after the final U-Haul was returned to Lincoln... leaving me and the kiddos alone. The security system for our "not-a-neighbor-in-sight" digs wouldn't be installed for at least two more weeks.

Now that may not sound like a big deal to some people, but you're talking to a woman who – in the past when her husband was traveling for work – used to survey the house from room to room with a kitchen knife and flashlight... terrified by bumps in the night and not having Mike by my side. I had gotten better since my kids were born, but still suffered from false-evidence-appearing-real (FEAR) syndrome, no thanks to daily doses of sensationalized "news" stories.

And, oh yeah, the Lord asked me to step out of my beloved Bible study. For 7+ years, I had enjoyed amazing fellowship and great spiritual transformation being part of a local branch of an international Bible study. I had a hard time believing that Jesus would ask me to leave this sisterhood of 300+ women that I had considered my extended family since we moved to Lincoln from Kalamazoo, Michigan. But along with the housing switch, Jesus was also telling me that a change was needed in all my relationships – including my relationship with Him.

Seriously, Lord?

It didn't seem logical to leave a BIBLE study, especially one that I had invested myself into so deeply! The 30+ minute lessons were my "go-to" for daily Quiet Time. The twice-weekly meetings made up my core friend group. And my 20+ hour weekly administrative position represented something akin to a part-time job, as I had been part of the leadership team since my second year of involvement.

During those first few months after the move, however, Jesus began to give me glimpses into why this seemingly topsy-turvy move was oh-so-right.

I realized that – during the last couple of years of Bible study group and unbeknownst to me during this time – my participation had warped from something spiritually transforming to relationship severing. Speaking the truth in love, Mike and both my children revealed to me what I was too blind to see: I had crossed over the line from serving in ministry to sacrificing family. I spent more time and prayer investing in "my ladies" than the three people who represented the greatest gifts that God could ever bless me with during my time on this Earth.

Worse of all, I realized that my relationship with Jesus was also affected by my jam-packed, regimented schedule. I had fallen prey to that nasty predator who threatens to overtake many-a-woman: OVERCOMMITMENT.

It may very well be the 8th deadly sin.

Amen, Sisters?

Between my part-time gig as Bible study class administrator and volunteer extraordinaire at both church and school, I had no slush time in my schedule whatsoever. I was meticulously mapping out – on paper, no less – every hour of the day, minute-by-minute. Anything outside the boundaries of this self-inflicted schedule prison either sent me into a dizzy of worry or an eruption of angry mama.

Basically, Jesus did for me what I didn't have the guts, strength or wisdom to do.

HE SAVED ME FROM MYSELF.

And redeemed my most precious relationships.

∾

A s I put the finishing touches on this chapter, Mike is happily out in the fields, shotgun in hand, looking to catch our next meal. But turkey dinner aside, I know Mike would agree the joy that he's now experiencing goes far beyond the original desire for hunting grounds. Clearly, our relocation has more to do with the Lord's pursuit of a deeper relationship with Mike, Chris, Chase and Mia. But really, this love story is not restricted to our family. Or country living. It doesn't matter whether your home is nestled on an acreage, centered downtown or tucked into a cozy cul-de-sac.

Jesus' love has no boundaries.

Our story is just one example of how a willingness to surrender to God's plans, no matter how seemingly unconventional, can result in something extraordinary.[3] I'm starting to see that "unconventional" is often a sure-fire cue of discerning that the voice speaking is Jesus! In contrast, the Enemy advocates a herd mentality, i.e. everyone else is so should you. This go-with-their-flow approach snuffs out the "good and pleasing and perfect" life that God desires for every individual.[4]

The Huether's still serve in church, school and community – but in healthy doses led by the Holy Spirit. In addition to a hubby cheerfully decked out in camo, I am living out my dream of becoming an author. My aspiring drummer son Chase is banging out his passion at all hours, i.e. no suburbia neighbors with napping babies. My daughter Mia continues to enjoy social time with friends, but is appreciating at an early age the value of a schedule that allows room to breathe.

Now I'm the one smiling, but not with sarcasm. Instead, my testimony is filled JOY – the joy of knowing the Lord more intimately than ever before. And the understanding that He loves me so much... God didn't just send His son to sacrifice His life on the cross for me... resurrect me along with Jesus from the dead... and provide me with eternal life with Him in heaven. That's certainly more than enough (and more than I deserve). But He also continues to save me daily here on Earth – like with something as wonderfully unsettling as a new address and restored relationships.

His methods may be uncommonly surprising at times.

Crazy in a God way.

And totally worth it.

---

1. God can do anything, you know—far more than you could ever imagine or guess or request in your wildest dreams! He does it not by pushing us around but by working within us, his Spirit deeply and gently within us. Glory to God in the church! Glory to God in the Messiah, in Jesus! Glory down all the generations! Glory through all millennia! Oh, yes! Ephesians 3:20-21 (MSG)

2. Cool story from the company's website about how U-Haul was founded! Check it out: https://www.uhaul.com/About/History/

3. "My thoughts are nothing like your thoughts," says the LORD. "And my ways are far beyond anything you could imagine. For just as the heavens are higher than the earth, so my ways are higher than your ways and my thoughts higher than your thoughts." Isaiah 55:8-9 (NLT)

4. Don't copy the behavior and customs of this world, but let God transform you into a new person by changing the way you think. Then you will learn to know God's will for you, which is good and pleasing and perfect. Romans 12:2 (NLT)

UNLISTED

People Power

My mind is swirling.

The head spins started after my 4AM "Quiet Time" with Jesus followed by "Alone Time" with my husband Mike – two of the most relationally intimate times of my day. If that isn't the work of Satan, then I don't know what is. Even now, two hours after I shouted "GOOD-BYE!" to my headed-off-to-work hubby through the steamy shower door, I find myself enslaved to distracting thoughts.

It's that darn To-Do List.

I don't know about you, but there is nothing about this sheet of paper or "Reminder" icon on my iMac® that I see as anything but self-defeating. Even when I do complete a task, I feel uncontrollably sucked into the next thing on the list. No mental confetti celebrating the most recent accomplishment. You know, "Good job, Chris!" "You go, girl!"

That would be nice, wouldn't it?

Instead, I'm left with my tattered paper sidekick, which is increasingly trashed with battle scars including coffee stains, warped pages and bent edges. And riddled with tiny pink scraps from my endless erases. (I learned long ago that writing in pen signifies a commitment to finish, which I can't ever seem to do, thanks to life's never-ending surprises. So I always opt to get the lead out, i.e. mechanical pencil, when adding an item or making changes.)

But I don't have just one centralized list.

I've got Post-it® notes and self-made reminders scribbled on a couple different notebooks, a Kleenex® on my dresser and a ripped off piece of newspaper on the kitchen counter. The "Reminder" app on my computer is separated into 16 sub-categories under the guise that – somehow – the more that I compartmentalize, the easier my life will become.

I have issues.

As I sit here on the bed, laptop in hand and Bible on the nightstand, I'm crying out to the Lord, *"Please, can I just finish one project today?"* Sometimes, I feel like the only thing that I accomplishment is un-accomplishment.

What's really pathetic?

Earlier this morning, I was immersed in an Easter devotional... meditating on the can't-even-get-my-brain-around sacrifice that Jesus made over 2,000 years ago for me. Everything I do embarrassingly pales in comparison to the love that Jesus demonstrated, not only on the cross but in the dailies of life.

Love shined as His #1 and only priority.

So how did Jesus and His apostles do it?

Somehow, they took care of the mundane yet seemingly necessities of life... and yet still loved their neighbors and, ultimately, the Lord with all their hearts, minds and strength.[1] The "stuff of life" had to be in there somewhere, right? Hitting the local marketplace for some grub.[2] Educating the kiddos academically, socially and, of course, spiritually. Throwing in a load of laundry. (With all the sweaty cross-country hikes and unavoidable olive oil spills, those tunics must have needed an occasional heavy-duty cleaning!) They were human, just like me.

So the question of the day:

How can love be my #1 to-do in the 21st century?[3]

As a homemaker who can't ignore the need to take care of food, shelter and clothing for her family. *As a wife* who desires to have dinner on the table when her knight returns home from office battles, while also be readily available (i.e. awake) to comfort him on the most intimate level. *As a mom* who knows time is running out on all the ways that she can train up her children to function independently – and in a God-honoring way – when they head out solo into this crazy world after high school? And as an *aspiring writer* who longs to share a few words of encouragement to other women... who sometimes, maybe like me, feel like throwing in the towel?

I'm not talking laundry here.

Lord, please help me![4]

~

T ime has passed.

But, honestly, I'm not sure how much.

I could have dozed off from the fumes of BIC Wite-Out®. (If I do hastily use a pen to add an item to my list, this correction fluid is my go-to when the inevitable moment comes to reprioritize and reorder a task or two.)

But I'm finally starting to hear His voice.

The voice of Wisdom.

I know Jesus is speaking to me, because the tone is oh-so-sweet.[5] More and more, I'm finding it easier to discern between the sound of my Savior and the Enemy. If I feel even a smidgeon of anxiety or stress, I know it's the bad guy attempting to finagle his twisted way into my desperately-seeking-peace brain. By twisted, I mean that he tries to redirect my thoughts away from God and towards me, i.e. Chris knows what's best.

No, thank you!

This morning, I'm not having it.

As always, Jesus is unmistakably kind – the signature mark of a message from my Best Friend. The Author of my salvation. The Creator of all things. The Lord over everything, including my To-Do List.

He's telling me to simply put others first.

So I'm looking at my list and thinking, yeah, I know this![6] That's another way that I can distinguish the voice of God from all others; it's perfectly in sync with what I read in Scripture. Thankfully, the Holy Spirit provides more specific direction that makes His command wonderfully clear: He's saying to flip the list... and put the last first. What does that mean today?

Write letters to my two sponsor children.[7]

This may sound terrible. But letters, thank you's, and other hand-written expressions often fall to the bottom of my list. I'm not really sure why I hesitate to enjoy these relational moments on paper, especially when – every time that I do – I am filled with an indescribable amount of JOY! Perhaps due to perfectionism or my profession, I've always felt that every word has to be "just so." I've been known to spend 30 minutes or more on crafting the perfect words on a 3 x 5" notecard. Or – gulp – an email. I fear saying something stupid or – more gulps – finding a typo later and looking like world's most inept writer.

Did I mention that I have issues?

Let it go, Chris.

By the way, that was Jesus speaking, not Idina Menzel.

Ok. Nuff said. Just the thought of doing this first makes me smile... and I feel a sense of fulfillment already. I glance at my list again. Second from the bottom?

Organize the tax information.

It's one of my most dreaded To-Do's, driven by a non-negotiable deadline – and one of my least favorite duties as the household manager. You know, it's one of those tasks (usually a monstrous one, from a time perspective) that you are continually shuffling down the list daily, trying to avoid, until finally – BOOM!

The deadline is less than 24 hours away.

And you are in BI-III-IG trouble.

April 15th is right around the corner. Three weeks ago, yes, I was waiting on information. Today, there is really no excuse. So I just can't put my finger on the reason – maybe just laziness or procrastination – why I simply can't seem to put on those finishing touches needed to seal up the envelope. And drop our paperwork off to Greg.

GREG.

Ok, I think I'm starting to get it. Although it seems like a no brainer, Jesus is giving me eyes to see. Jesus is sharing His vision. *Literally.* He's putting a *face* on everything that's before me. Because for every seemingly cold, dry word on my To-Do List, there is someone – *a human being created in His image* – that will be affected by my decision to either delve right in.

Or let it sit.

Yikes.

I really like our CPA, Greg. And when I think about him, I feel gratefulness welling up inside of me. It sounds so simple. However, I quickly become overwhelmed when looking at what seems like the endless responsibilities in front of me. That's when my thoughts get swallowed up by a cram-in-as-much-done-as-possible mentality. In other words, the more I cross off my list – and the faster – the better.

But the better for *what*?

And for *who*?

Take Greg, for example. Yes, I have considered "what if" every one of his clients handed in their taxes three weeks out – or a few days before the April 15 deadline. (Sadly, in the past, I have been one of "those people.") But the Lord is not about that – that being guilt and shame! Those are two words that you won't find in the Kingdom dictionary. Ever since I grabbed hold of Jesus as my Savior, my proverbial slate is now – and will always – be clean. His desire and intention is always offering up a reset. (And, believe me, I take Him up on that gracious offer several times daily!)

So today, He's telling me to stop trying to tackle my To-Do's. Instead, Jesus says to envision each item on my list as an opportunity to make a difference. Not in the world, necessarily.

But in the life of one person.

So, it really isn't the "big picture" approach, is it... like the tired-old secular cliché? It's more of a microscopic zoom. Every one of the To-Do's on my list *does* matter – and from a Kingdom perspective – it all comes down to one reason: PEOPLE. Not a sense of accomplishment. Or a race to get as many things checked off as possible. It's not even for the sake of being altruistic.

It's for the glory of God.

Because God is love.[8]

Jesus was the only one in history who *always* put people first. And because He was God in the flesh, we have a pretty darn good idea what is #1 on the Father's To-Do List.

Only Jesus can free me from the chains of the mundane... and turn what seems like a simple To-Do into something God-ordained and beautiful. In doing so, He is also transforming this formerly performance-driven gal into a relationship-lovin' mama. In the end, I'll be doing my part in helping to bring the Kingdom of God and His love to Earth right now.

One to-do at a time.

So I guess you could say I've been official "unlisted," in terms of my old way of thinking about the dailies. No more drowning in the doing.

I'm swimming against the Tide®.

Trusting in the power of the Holy Spirit to help me put people first... while also believing that God – in His perfect timing – will enable me to take care of the stuff of life.[9]

Like clean socks and underwear.

For the love of God!

Amen.

---

1. Jesus replied, "You must love the Lord your God with all your heart, all your soul, and all your mind." Matthew 22:37 (NLT)

2. There's a mention in John 4:8 that the disciples left Jesus to head into the city to buy food. Therefore, we know that some type of grocery shopping occasionally made its way on the To-Do lists in New Testament times, too!

3. Imitate God, therefore, in everything you do, because you are his dear children. Live a life filled with love, following the example of Christ. He loved us and offered himself as a sacrifice for us, a pleasing aroma to God. Ephesians 5:1-2 (NLT)

4. Do any of you need wisdom? Ask God for it. He is generous and enjoys giving to everyone. So he will give you wisdom. James 1:5 (ERV)

5. But the wisdom that comes from God is like this: First, it is pure. It is also peaceful, gentle, and easy to please. This wisdom is always ready to help people who have trouble and to do good for others. This wisdom is always fair and honest. James 3:17 (ERV)

6. Don't look out only for your own interests, but take an interest in others, too. Philippians 2:4 (NLT)

7. https://www.compassion.com

8. Dear friends, let us continue to love one another, for love comes from God. Anyone who loves is a child of God and knows God. But anyone who does not love does not know God, for God is love. 1 John 4:7-8 (NLT)

9. Dear friends, since God loved us that much, we surely ought to love each other. No one has ever seen God. But if we love each other, God lives in us, and his love is brought to full expression in us. 1 John 4:11-12 (NLT)

NO BLIND SPOTS

County Road 13

Once again, the Lord divinely intervened to prevent an earthly tragedy in our family's life.

I emphasize *once again,* because I have evidence demonstrating how He's saved us over the past few months. Earlier this year, the Lord led me to start a list of all the God moments.[1] For the record, I'm running out of space on my journal's pages.

Or it could also mean that this middle-aged mama is so prone to disaster, only massive doses of heavenly assistance will keep her alive.

On any note, yesterday's saving grace is another example – or better described as proof positive – of supernatural protection that a sinner like me certainly doesn't deserve. And yet the Lord keeps rescuing me and my loved ones, especially when it comes to the Huether vehicles, because of His mercy. As I reflect back on yesterday, I could define it as a DUHI.

Spiritually speaking, that is.

Driving Under His Influence.

∾

As we headed into the Southpoint Mall parking lot, my son Chase was sharing his enthusiasm about his latest book with me. (He's an avid reader way beyond his years; the dude read "Unbroken" as a 5th grade homeschooler in less than three days. Seriously. I love this guy.) I treasure these one-on-one moments, especially knowing that I have only five short years remaining with this amazing young man.[2]

I made a quick left turn into the parking lot, in search of a spot close to a local optical shop, where I hoped the missing pad on my eyeglasses could be easily replaced. When I woke up this morning, it was mysteriously gone. I suspect some canine intervention, as both my Huskies enjoy chewies that can't be found in any pet store – underwear, pencils, dental floss and other delicacies that make the traditional sock steal look like amateur play.

The ever-so-tiny clear nose piece doesn't seem that critical – until you lose it. At that point, the word "spectacle" takes on a whole new meaning. Limping along with one pad vs. two, my eyeglasses had taken on an uncomfortable seesaw effect; their teetering on my nose was wreaking havoc on both my style (yeah, like I really have one!) and skin.

But God had plans beyond fixing my earthly vision challenges. I was about to see Proverb 16:9 come to life (before my very impaired eyes, that is):

We can make our plans, but the Lord determines our steps.

As I turned the vehicle, I made eye contact with a stranger in an SUV, who silently mouthed something to me. I pulled up alongside a woman who – little did I know at the time – could later be described as a verifiable guardian angel. She shared that my back tire was almost completely flat.

At that moment, I thought "Darn my love for driving on low

maintenance country roads!" The culprit behind the flat was most certainly County Road 13[3].

Only two roads lead to our secluded abode on the outskirts of civilization. The first one, County Road 13, is wrought with all sorts of non-traditional obstacles. (Just visualize an oversized bike trail.) This single-lane dirt road presents the possibility of meeting head-to-head with another vehicle, which could require strategically backing up all the way to the start, i.e. up to 1/2 mile in the "Reverse" mode. It also offers an occasional wild animal sighting... trek over a widely-slatted wooden bridge... and bumpy ride across ruts of eroded soil up to 6 inches deep.

Why does this sound fun to me?!

Sane human beings choose the second route: County Road 14. This gravel-covered option is plenty wide enough for two vehicles. Plus it's scrupulously maintained by our beloved Otoe County grader. This nameless yet oh-so-kind man, who always gives the one-finger-lift-off-the-steering-wheel country wave while driving by our house, has graciously plowed the Huether family out of many a snowstorm.

County Road 13 does, however, have one advantage. Despite the treacherous drive, it's about 3 minutes faster.

Just saying!

Hence, the challenge: In order to reach trusty #14, I have to drive pass naughty #13. EVERY DAY. Oh, darn that beast called Temptation, who relentlessly attempts to lure me down a seemingly easier but always bad path!

Two weeks ago, I vowed to never drive down County Road 13 again, after experiencing a similar nearly-flat tire. On that morning, after I said goodbye to my kids in the school's drop-off loop, the principal bravely stepped in front of my moving vehicle and alerted me to a potentially life-threatening situation. Same tire. I was wise enough to set aside my agenda – and immediately drove to the local Honda dealer for a quick fix. Although I'm not

100% certain that County Road 13 was the culprit behind that puncture, I guess it's certainly within the realm of possibility. So I told myself "Never again!" to #13. I even attempted to seal the deal by announcing my solemnly-swear oath to my husband Mike, who seemed reluctant to believe his off-road lovin' wife.

But alas! Temptation, once again, proved too great.

Yesterday, I rationalized that it *was* a tad bit faster – and *would* add a sense of adventure to this homemaker's day, especially after a hum-drum grocery run.

I mean, *what could it hurt?*

Right now, my empty promise to travel rightly was taking its toll in the mall parking lot. I decided I'd better let Jesus take the wheel. Obviously, my judgment has not been 100% reliable.

I am not a split-second thinker. However, without hesitation, I didn't stop to examine the situation – or decide to leave the tire "as is" until after my eyeglass fix. Instead, I told Chase that our plans had changed; we'd be heading to a nearby gas station. My mind wandered, for just a second, to what the tire looked like.

Will we make it?

But God-confidence forced out any trace of doubt... and I wisely continued to follow His rescue plan.[4]

Suddenly, I heard a ring.

I handed my iPhone over to Chase, since I was driving and – honestly – already quite distracted. Mike was on the other end of the line. Chase explained the tire situation to him, but unfortunately threw in that Mom... just a few minutes ago after he finished his last of six Nacho Cheese Doritos Locos Tacos®... pulled her own locos move. Ok, so I *may* have driven our SUV over a small – *really, it was insignificant in size* – curb next to Taco Bell®. "I'M SURE THAT HAD NOTHING TO DO WITH IT!"... I loudly shouted into the conversation, while leaning over towards Chase from the driver's side.

I soon tuned out the incriminating rap session between my

two favorite men, as our vehicle approached the Shell® gas station. "YES!" I exclaimed. I was tempted to add a celebratory fist pump. But since I was already looking darn-right pathetic in the driving area, I kept both hands on the steering wheel. Then I saw an air pump on the side of the building, just a few yards ahead of us, flanked by two open parking spots.

Praise the Lord!

My "YES" made a quick change into "Saaay WHAT?" An odd-looking antique sports car, appeared to have been flattened by Goliath no less, zipped into what had looked like our flat tire refuge. It didn't just take up one parking spot. This smashed-down motorized carrot managed to dangle itself in the middle of the painted yellow line, greedily calling dibs of the entire area in direct proximity to the air pump.

SERIOUSLY?

Chase shut off the cell phone. Handed it back to me. Then shared that Dad said to fill up the tire at the gas station; he would meet us there shortly. I felt my God-confidence kick into high gear again. I turned the steering wheel in what seemed like a heavenly autopilot. The clock read 5:25PM. The Honda dealer, located a few blocks down the street, was open for five more minutes. I'd like to call it an executive decision, but it definitely wasn't of the earthly "Chris" kind. (We've seen where her decisions lead, 'nuf said.) In this case, the Executive was the Holy Spirit, living inside me. This free gift from God has been my wise guide, ever since I confessed my sins and accepted Jesus as my Savior just a little over five years ago.[5]

We pulled up to the garage door of the Honda service station. Before we could even stop the vehicle, the giant steel panels lifted slowly up. We pulled inside. The staff graciously agreed to look at the tire, despite the fact that the dealer was officially closing in three minutes. And, much to my surprise, they removed a screw from our nearly 100% flat tire.

In about 10 minutes.

For a mere 20 dollars.

From the perspective of anyone blind to the love of Christ, it was no miracle. Merely happenstance. Bad fortune luckily fixed. An unforeseen incident with a chance happy ending.

Come on.

Let's get real.

I know what just happened here!!

The original plan was Dad would meet Chase and me at Southpoint Mall. The boys would head home in Dad's vehicle... while I waited to pick up my daughter Mia after an all-day school field trip. We girls would make the 25-minute voyage home in pitch-darkness via Highway 2 – the same highway that I traveled just two hours ago only to witness a three-car collision with a slew of emergency vehicles and injured people. If not for the Holy Spirit's guidance, a horrific scene like that one could have very well been me and Mia later tonight. Or this I've-never-changed-a-tire woman and her sweet 9-year-old girl could have been stranded on the highway or a remote country road.

Fortunately, the Lord is not just omnipresent.[6] He is also actively involved in the lives of His helpless people. Even a woman who makes a very wrong choice (ok, let's call it for what it is – STUPID) to repeatedly drive down one of those low maintenance roads "just for fun."

I'm thankful that His idea of fun is not the same as mine.

～

What's one of the best revelations from this just-another-one-of-His-countless-saving-grace moments? Without doubt, the Lord protected my daughter and me from a situation that could have definitely been physically and emotionally harrowing!

But I also love how He gives me eyes to see victories in the unseen battles that swirl all around me. As a Christ follower, I know that spiritual blindness is – by far – the most dangerous road hazard in our journey through this foreign land, i.e. our earthly existence, en route to our heavenly home. I'm not ashamed to say that I'm saved by faith in Jesus and will join him in Paradise one day![7]

But why wait?

Why miss out on the euphoria of seeing the endless miracles that God performs every day? Some people come to know Jesus as Savior in their final days – perhaps even in their last breath. That's amazing! Of course, the angels in heaven sing with joy when any formerly lost soul finally realizes the Truth and shouts out a resounding "YES!"

However, a final-hour countdown is not for me.

I want to revel in the wonder of all His glory NOW.[8]

As I wrap up another story of God's mercy and grace, I have but one prayer: NO BLIND SPOTS. Oh, Lord, help me see more of you everywhere! I resolve to be on lookout for more God moments, which reveal that there is no such thing as mere physical coincidences. Spiritual realities do exist, like the one that my family experienced today, which offer glorious proof that God is with us. He is for us. And, unlike the flat tires of this life, He is offering the only life filled heavenly bliss.

In the meantime, I will stay off Country Road 13.

I promise?

Thank you, Lord, that *your* promises are legit.[9]

---

1. O Lord my God, you have performed many wonders for us. Your plans for us are too numerous to list. You have no equal. If I tried to recite all your wonderful deeds, I would never come to the end of them. Psalm 40:5 (NLT)
2. Teach us to realize the brevity of life, so that we may grow in wisdom. Psalm 90:12 (NLT)

3. The names have been changed to protect the innocent or – more specifically – those of you sweet readers who could also be lured into the strange not-so-good-for-me appeal of the low maintainance country roads. In other words, don't even go there, Sisters!

4. For the Lord grants wisdom! From his mouth come knowledge and understanding. Proverbs 2:6 (NLT)

5. And now you Gentiles have also heard the truth, the Good News that God saves you. And when you believed in Christ, he identified you as his own by giving you the Holy Spirit, whom he promised long ago. Ephesians 1:13 (NLT)

6. I can never escape from your Spirit! I can never get away from your presence! If I go up to heaven, you are there; if I go down to the grave, you are there. If I ride the wings of the morning, if I dwell by the farthest oceans, even there your hand will guide me, and your strength will support me. Psalm 139:7-10 (NLT)

7. For I am not ashamed of this Good News about Christ. It is the power of God at work, saving everyone who believes—the Jew first and also the Gentile. Romans 1:16 (NLT)

8. Jesus said, "But if you don't believe me when I tell you about earthly things, how can you possibly believe if I tell you about heavenly things?" John 3:12 (NLT)

9. God's way is perfect. All the Lord's promises prove true. He is a shield for all who look to him for protection. Psalm 18:30 (NLT)

HELL OR HEAVEN

You Decide

How do I stop myself from being sucked back into hell?

That was the inscription on the lime green sticky note, which I scribbled last night and posted on my desktop.

I wrote it at the end of a particularly "trying" yesterday, which started with an unexpected medical report and wrapped up with a 13-year-old sulking up to bed. I didn't want to miss delving into this question a little deeper during my next early morning Quiet Time.

So here I am ready for Wisdom.

Fireplace flickering. Java in hand. (I like to snatch the first cup drenched in grounds while the coffee pot is still brewing – that's the key to my morning acceleration into consciousness. Gotta love that pause-and-brew feature!) I'm armed with Bible Gateway on my iPad along with my preciously-worn NLT hard copy. Plus there's the Easter devotion that I've been reading and meditating on, as of late, titled *Jesus Keep Me Near the Cross.*[1]

I pray to the Holy Spirit for enlightenment... then begin to ponder the somewhat cryptic words on the Post-It® note.

Jesus, what are you trying to teach me?

ST. E'S HOSPITAL PARKING LOT

Yesterday morning, my annual 30-minute "routine" mammogram morphed into three hours, which included extra images and a one-on-one meeting with Dr. B in an off-the-beaten-path room staring at my breasts on the big screen.

Long story short?

A stereotactic biopsy was promptly scheduled.[2]

I exited the hospital's side doors. Walked up to the 3rd floor of the parking ramp. Then slipped into my vehicle driver's seat, seemingly as usual. That's when the 180-minute mental rollercoaster ride came to a screeching halt. I was dumbstruck by a situation that could only be described as surreal.

Wow.

This is happening.

THIS... is happening... to ME.

I tried not to cry.

I wasn't playing the blame game with God. Or questioning His plans on the potentially cancerous cells. Instead, I found myself confused.

Why do I feel like crying? I know that You love me, Jesus. I believe You! I'm know that You're in control of all of this!!

That's when it hit me.

I was under attack.[3]

The Enemy of my soul recognized that I could be vulnerable. He was tempting me to doubt my Savior. I'm talking about the Liar. That's one of Satan's titles referred to in the Bible, which describes a key characteristic of his nature. His number one mission? Separating me (and you) from the truth of God's love, the only remedy for surviving and thriving in the midst of unexpected turn-of-events.

Like the potential of breast cancer.

At that moment, I realized the only way that I could fight this battle was by aligning my thoughts with God's. Remembering all the Truths that I had immersed myself in for the past few years. And applying those Truths to my situation.

Right here.

I bowed my head into the steering wheel... then vowed not to be swept away by "what if's." As I began to pray, any flirtation with doubting my Savior began to fade.[4]

As I focused on listening to Jesus' gentle whispers, I stepped out of the darkness that Satan was dangling in front of me: His lies that my situation was hopeless... and I should leave this parking lot in bitterness. Instead, I felt as if the doors of heaven opened up and Jesus' light washed over me: The truth that God is good... He loves me... and I can trust Him. Best of all, Jesus has guaranteed me a glorious future with Him for all eternity – whether the cells are cancerous or not.

Then I boogied to the Dunkin' Donuts® drive-through to indulge in a large Caramel Swirl Macchiato. Now that's a victory celebration over doubt done right, Amen?

I'm convinced it was Jesus' idea.

He knows what He's doing!

THE HUETHER KITCHEN

Last night, my son Chase and I had a little "heated" conversation. 'Nuf said. But when Chase's voice seemed to reach a straining point, I did not feel that tired-old sensation of going it solo. And getting it all so very wrong.

In days gone by, "*Why can't I stop myself from doing this?!*" was my helpless cry. My default position was involuntarily doing the opposite of what I knew was right! "*Why did I just say that?!!*" As if I had no control whatsoever, ill-chosen words coated with a harsher-than-intended tone spilled from my mouth. Scrunched-up eyebrows set in a stony face were additional tell-tale signs that this woman was *not* tapping into the Holy Spirit.

I can honestly say that our family doesn't fight with each other anymore – at least not like we used to do. Yes, we still encounter some differences in opinion. But I've been told those not-on-the-same-wavelength moments are what help us grow, whether you're a Jesus follower or "no-go" to Christianity.

For the most part, verbal blowouts are gone. No more relationships painfully scorched with self-inflicted wounds, followed by the lingering scars of guilt and shame. Now instead of disagreements seeped in emotional chaos – both during and afterwards – the Holy Spirit is blessing me with His divine gifts, including patience, gentleness and self-control.[5]

Essentially, over the past few months and years, the Lord has been laying the foundation... helping me to prepare for last night... for that moment when the Holy Spirit would empower me to look Chase straight in the eyes with the goal of healing and unity. What absolute joy to say goodbye to the Devil's methodology of looking away, which fuels self-focus and pride.

I've been there.

Done the latter.

And so hated the damage inflicted not only on my own soul, but also my relationships. As we hang out together every morning, Jesus is teaching me how the Holy Spirit can work through me to fight *for* my relationships *in His strength alone* versus my imperfect human attempts at sin management!

While Chase was speaking to me, I was looking in his eyes and listening more intently than ever before. Sure, those two things could also be said of secular approaches to conflict resolution. But unlike worldly ways, I was also *praying and meditating* on how much I *deeply love* this extraordinary young man – instead of strategizing on how to make my point or win the war.

No doubt, there was a war taking place at the kitchen

counter last night. But it was a spiritual battle between good and evil. Thankfully, I employed the Armor of God versus flimsy secular shields, like gritting my teeth.[6] Jesus continues to free me daily from sin and its nasty consequences, including damaged relationships.

He's also helping me avoid costly dental bills.

~

Soooo… this morning, I find myself thankful for the reminder – both yesterday morning and last night – on one thing that I often take for granted:

I'm not alone.

No matter where I am.

Because of Jesus and my faith in him, I can now come boldly and confidently into God's presence.[7] But our get-togethers don't just take place in the wee hours of the morning. At the moment that I said "Yes!" to His invite to be my forever Savior, Jesus promised to be with me, every second of every day. A divine 24/7 FaceTime®, so to speak, that continues not only through my short time on Earth, but also my permanent home in Heaven.

With all that being said, wouldn't the opposite ring true?

You're either with Him. Or without Him.

You choose heaven. Or hell.

What is hell? It's separation from God. The Bible affirms that after physical death, an eternal separation from God is awaiting those who chose not to believe.[8] Yesterday, I was reminded of how it isn't just an after-earth reality.

Hell can exist right here and now.

I got a disturbing glimpse when tempted in the hospital parking lot. A smidgeon of reminder in the Huether kitchen. But the most profound "Ah-ha" of all? For the overwhelming majority of my earthly life, I sadly *chose to go it alone* and live separated from all His goodness. I can only imagine how yesterday's parking lot scene would have played out if the "old Chris" was in the driver's seat. Or if she forced her way into the kitchen last night.

YIKES doesn't even come close to describing it.

I realize now the formidable word on that Post-it note was not "back." Going back is no longer a possibility. That's because I have the glorious, unlimited resources and inner strength of His Holy Spirit, living inside me.[9] This Spirit is not only an incredible reminder of the 100% guarantee of my destiny, but also the wisest always-on-call Counselor of all time.[10] ("Duh" seems appropriate here, because this Spirit is from God Himself.)[11] He gives the right advice for every relationship scenario and personal dilemma.

So if my son wakes up sulking, I'll give him a hug. And when I show up for the biopsy after dropping off my kids at school? I'll slip on that hospital gown knowing, without doubt, God doesn't just have my back. He's got my present and my future, too.

WOW doesn't even begin to describe it!

So my final read between the original Post-it note lines? It's not the *how* that will stop me from being "sucked into hell."

It's the *Who*.

He'll be with me this afternoon when a sample of my breast tissue is surgically removed. (When I said earlier that the biopsy was promptly scheduled, I meant *this afternoon* – less than 24 hours after the mammogram.)

Heaven is real.

His name is Jesus.

When you choose to believe, separation from Him is impossible. It simply ain't happening. Ever. And the word "alone"?

It becomes divinely obsolete.

---

1. *Jesus, Keep Me Near the Cross: Experiencing the Passion and Power of Easter*, is a collection of readings drawn from the writings and sermons of 25 classic and contemporary theologians and Bible teachers, focusing on the wonder of Christ's sacrifice. Edited by Nancy Guthrie (Illinois: Crossway Books, 2009)

2. A stereotactic breast biopsy is an outpatient procedure that uses computer technology to guide a needle to an abnormality seen on mammography.

3. Stay alert! Watch out for your great enemy, the devil. He prowls around like a roaring lion, looking for someone to devour. 1 Peter 5:8 (NLT)

4. So humble yourselves before God. Resist the devil, and he will flee from you. James 4:7 (NLT)

5. But the Holy Spirit produces this kind of fruit in our lives: love, joy, peace, patience, kindness, goodness, faithfulness, gentleness, and self-control. There is no law against these things! Galatians 5:22-23 (NLT)

6. Therefore, put on every piece of God's armor so you will be able to resist the enemy in the time of evil. Then after the battle you will still be standing firm. Stand your ground, putting on the belt of truth and the body armor of God's righteousness. For shoes, put on the peace that comes from the Good News so that you will be fully prepared. In addition to all of these, hold up the shield of faith to stop the fiery arrows of the devil. Put on salvation as your helmet, and take the sword of the Spirit, which is the word of God. Pray in the Spirit at all times and on every occasion. Stay alert and be persistent in your prayers for all believers everywhere. Ephesians 6:13-18 (NLT)

7. Ephesians 3:12 (NLT)

8. But cowards, unbelievers, the corrupt, murderers, the immoral, those who practice witchcraft, idol worshipers, and all liars—their fate is in the fiery lake of burning sulfur. This is the second death. Revelation 21:8 (NLT)

9. I pray that from his glorious, unlimited resources he will empower you with inner strength through his Spirit. Then Christ will make his home in your hearts as you trust in him. Your roots will grow down into God's love and keep you strong. Ephesians 3:16-17 (NLT)

10. The Spirit is God's guarantee that he will give us the inheritance he promised and that he has purchased us to be his own people. He did this so we would praise and glorify him. Ephesians 1:14 (NLT)

11. Don't you realize that your body is the temple of the Holy Spirit, who lives in you and was given to you by God? 1 Corinthians 6:19 (NLT)

JOY RIDE

Highway 2

I hope I don't pass out.

That thought crossed my mind, as the kids and I pulled out of our gravel driveway at 7:15AM and headed down the country road for our 25-minute trek to school. Yesterday, I passed out after the stereotactic breast biopsy at St. E's Hospital.

I've never fainted before.

Nearly 24 hours had passed since my consciousness stepped out for a while. That seems like enough recuperation time, right? But for whatever reason, whether the lingering memory of the previous day's events or the after-procedure tenderness in my left breast, I was definitely feeling out of it.

"24 divided by 6 is 4..."

Those numbers jolted me back to reality.

Mia had begun reciting her Rocket Math®.

It's a daily exercise that helps elementary students practice and master math facts. In one minute, Mia reads math problems on a worksheet – as fast as she can – plus provides the correct answers. If more than two wrong answers, she starts back at the beginning and repeats the process all over again. Like the extreme opposite of counting sheep at night to help one fall asleep, my 9-year-old daughter's recitation of Rocket Math every morning during our drive to school served as a mental launch into her upcoming 8-hour shift in academia.

Truth be told?

Completion of this daily homework also ensured that Mia would get her fix of a handful of M&M's®, which was provided by her 4th grade teacher as an incentive.

SCREW THE LIFE SKILLS!

Just hand over the sweets.

I'm sensing that I'm trailing off in terms of Biblical direction.

Back to the SUV.

The repetition of numbers was making me space out. And I'm not talking extraterrestrial here. Rather that darn demon known as Worry was threatening to – should I say – school me! Fear was insidiously creeping into my thoughts. I began asking myself the following question, which was essentially a moot point because we were already well en route to our destination:

Should I be driving the kids to school this morning?

"36 divided by 4 is 9... Done!"

From the back seat, Mia declared victory – and undoubtedly freedom – as Rocket Math is not just an exercise in knowledge, but could also be defined as a test of one's personal sanity (both hers and mine). Depending on your frame of mind at the time, the mundane recitation of 40+ equations – although admittedly helpful academically – could be mentally akin to pulling out one's teeth, one by one.

I enthusiastically commended my studious daughter with a "Well done, Sister!" while sneaking a peak in the rearview mirror at my tween drummer Chase, who was – as usual – tapping out a beat on his knee, ear buds in place, staring out the window perhaps imagining future cross-country trips in a white tour van with his dream band.

I smiled thinking how much I love these crazy-cool kids. But

Satan quickly finagled his way back in my mental picture. I found myself entangled in the following notion:

I hope it isn't stupid to be driving...

I slowed down as our vehicle approached the stop sign – a visual marker of where easy-going gravel intersects with a 65mph asphalt ascent into civilization. At that precise moment, these words spilled out of my mouth in the form of a song:

Do not fear for I am with you. Do not be afraid... for I am your God. I will strengthen you and help you. I will uphold you with my righteous... my righteous right hand. [1]

It happened so spontaneously, with no seemingly conscious forethought. My head jerked backward a bit. Eyes popped open a little wider. And my former teetering-on-the-edge-of-madness disposition felt instantly renewed, as if splashed with a refreshing blast of spiritual cool.

In other words, He got my attention.

I couldn't remember the exact place in the Bible where this passage was located... maybe Joshua? But it didn't really matter. I was immediately comforted, as His Words trickled down from my head into my heart. Chase and Mia couldn't hear me; they were deep in the midst of their melodic cerebral preparation. In other words, they were listening to a favorite playlist on their iPod touches®, anticipating the upcoming rigors of elementary and junior high, respectively.

I replied to His divine message:

You're right, Jesus.

Then the light bulb kicked on.

I had memorized this verse years ago, when I first declared Jesus as my Savior and understood that memorizing Scripture was vital to soul revival. Apparently, these words of Truth had been hidden in my heart. Jesus was intentionally blessing me with this heavenly memory recall. He had heard my cries for help, even when I didn't even think to pray. In retrospect, I realized that I probably should have been praying vs. worrying in the first place!

The last time that I actively applied this specific passage of Scripture was over six years ago. At that time, I was reciting these verses to my then 1st-grade son at bedtime, shortly after the Lord moved our family to Lincoln – and just a few months after the Holy Spirit opened my eyes to my need for the Savior. I felt God leading me to pray this Scripture over Chase. I saw this Bible passage as Jesus' way of personally working through me to help my *"I am not comfortable in this place yet"* son begin to see that this unfamiliar city would soon feel like home.

It's possible that I may have thought of this Scripture *some time* since those early days. But I certainly don't remember seeing this Bible reference in my daily devotional or hearing these Words at any teaching at our church recently. Yet at that moment in the SUV, when I needed something beyond my own strength, the Lord mercifully rescued me with the gift of His peace.[2]

Well, it was peaceful for a while.

How soon I would forget. No wonder God hammers home the importance of remembering His faithfulness in over 60 verses throughout the Bible!

A few minutes later on Highway 2, I became self-focused again. Always a "no-no" when peace is the goal. I was mentally strategizing what I would do if I began to feel dizzy while driving down the road:

Maybe I shouldn't be using cruise control? That way, if I pass out, the vehicle will slowly come to a stop on its own. Then I could press the emergency lights button...

After I came up with "My Plan," the mental torment continued. (Surprise, surprise!) I was definitely getting a taste of why the Lord commands us repeatedly not to worry. In fact, I recall reading somewhere that references to "do not fear" and "do not worry" appear over 365 times in the Bible.[3]

So why was I doing this to myself?!

Perhaps the silence in the vehicle, with the kids zoning out on their music, could have attributed to my relapse. (Not blaming, just speculating.) No matter how hard I tried to stop it, I couldn't stop thinking about the possibility of an accident.

I turned on the radio as a final attempt at peace.

The deejays on our local Christian radio were quizzing the audience to see what was "the number four thing that people have in their junk drawer." *Screwdriver!!* I'm certain of it! It feels good to – at least temporarily – force my mind down the proverbial bunny trail. After a few minutes of that temporarily effective distraction, I heard the radio announcers say, "And today's Verse of the day...."

> *Do not fear for I am with you. Do not be afraid for I am your God. I will strengthen you and help you. I will uphold you with my righteous right hand.*[4]

I breathed in the reality of His intoxicating grace... felt my heart wildly race by the awareness of His loving presence... and sensed every smidgen of stress melt from my face, only to be replaced with a smile that could not be contained. The only thought in my mind at that moment?

Thank you, Jesus.

Although the naysayers of this world would undoubtedly believe otherwise, I know the Truth. Those perfectly-timed words were sent by the God of the Universe.

Just for me.

I don't profess to know *how* He does it. God's sovereignty and omniscience, that is. Omniscience (which I confess I still occasionally mispronounce) is a "big" word for His ability to know everything about everybody all the time. Of course, I realize that hundreds of other people were listening to the radio at that moment, too. But somehow, miraculously and mysteriously, the Creator of the Universe has the power to speak into every one of His children's lives in an amazingly intimate way – like He just did for me. I can't even begin to understand this kind of super-natural and unconditionally crazy-kind-of Love.

That's not just wishful thinking.

It's the reality of the Living Word.

And I'm listening!

~

Once and for all, I left Worry and Fear behind at the Bennet exit – our halfway marker to school. As we turned onto 98th Street heading into Lincoln, I began to chuckle recalling how my son recently teased me about my extensive library of Scripture memory CDs. The total number? Seventeen, no less!

My love for music inspired by Scripture dates back to 2006, when the Lord revealed I was a sinner in need of a Savior. I felt helplessly in need of immersing myself in His Word, but I just couldn't develop a routine for memorizing verses. Then the Lord led me to God Rocks®[5] and Mark Altrogge's Hide the Word®.[6] These ministries put Bible verses to catchy instrumental music. With these awesome tools in hand (or ears, is more like it), anyone can experience the joy of memorizing God's Word.[7]

Originally, my goal was accelerated life change and prepara-tion for crisis situations. (Yup, I was one of those fatalistic thinking kind of gals.) But the music was so enjoyable and uplifting, I found myself listening while driving in the car, running on the treadmill, walking the dogs and making dinner.

(Ok, "making dinner" is admittedly a stretch in my case. I was likely sticking a frozen pizza in the oven. But, hey! That's still a seven minute wait while cooking! And plenty of time for a little heavenly tuneage.)

Another benefit? Chase and Mia were in their early elementary years when I started jammin' to the Good News. Unwittingly, I turned my Honda Pilot into a mobile musical mission field. In addition to Mom's spiritual growth, two precious little souls were also being seeped in God's Word. Three minds renewed for the price of one Spiritual groove. I'm talking everywhere we traveled together including school, grocery store and more. Do the math: That's at least 7 hours each week "singing psalms and hymns and spiritual songs to God with thankful hearts." Colossians 3:16 in action![8]

Best of all, this is nothing I planned.

God made it happen.

And I absolutely love Him for it.

Today, Chase and Mia may not be able to remember a given Bible reference. But, in terms of Scripture, my kids can definitely sing out His words. And that makes this *"formerly unchurched for over 43 years and no way in hell do I want my kids to go through what I did!"* redeemed Mama smile.

Or maybe I should just belt out 1 John 3:1.[9]

See?

It's working.

Today I'm more inclined to listen to Casting Crowns, Rebecca St. James and other artists, whose works are inspired by verses in the Bible. Many of these artists even write down the Scripture reference behind their songs, which I find incredibly encouraging as I listen to them daily.

So let the world tease, even my own family.

Because no doubt, when I take the time to memorize His words – somewhere down the line – He will bring that Scripture into my life at just the perfect time.[10] And hearing Jesus' voice through Scripture – whether reading my Bible in the morning or recalling His words during my day at divinely-ordained moments – is the next best thing to Him physically being here.

Today, Jesus took the hell out of my ride.

And filled it with joy instead.

Plus I'm still alive to sing about it.

———

1. Isaiah 41:10 (NIV)
2. Jesus said, "I am leaving you with a gift—peace of mind and heart. And the peace I give is a gift the world cannot give. So don't be troubled or afraid." John 14:27 (NLT)
3. A great example of these 365 references? Check out these words spoken by Jesus in Matthew 6:31-33 (NLT): "So don't worry about these things, saying, 'What will we eat? What will we drink? What will we wear?' These things dominate the thoughts of unbelievers, but your heavenly Father already knows all your needs. Seek the Kingdom of God above all else, and live righteously, and he will give you everything you need."
4. Yup. That would be Isaiah 41:10 again. (NIV)
5. https://www.jellytelly.com/series/god-rocks-music-videos
6. http://www.forevergratefulmusic.com
7. I take joy in doing your will, my God, for your instructions are written on my heart. Psalm 40:8 (NLT)
8. Let the message about Christ, in all its richness, fill your lives. Teach and counsel each other with all the wisdom he gives. Sing psalms and hymns and spiritual songs to God with thankful hearts. Colossians 3:16 (NLT)
9. Check out the song "How Great," which reminds me of John 3:1, featured on the album *Glory Revealed II - The Word of God in Worship*. Songwriters: Mac Powell, Trevor Morgan, and Johnny Powell.
10. It is the same with my word. I send it out, and it always produces fruit. It will accomplish all I want it to, and it will prosper everywhere I send it. Isaiah 55:11 (NLT)

COINCIDENCE?

Not a Chance

A fter dropping off my kiddos at school, I was peacefully cruising down Highway 2 making the 25-minute return trip to our country home. I was experiencing one of those rare moments in motherhood when your brain enjoys a temporary shutdown. It's that blissful numbness of a mind freed from responsibilities and the usual, non-stop inner monologue about what to tackle next on "the list."

I was immersed in my favorite worship music... streaming at its loudest volume and filling every inch of my SUV's interior... unabashedly singing at the top of my lungs... without a second thought to ear damage or the possibility of strangers in passing vehicles glancing over and thinking "that woman is losing it."

Just living in the moment.

Ahh...

No strategizing about what needs to be done when I walk in the mudroom door upon returning home. No mind wandering into worries that I cannot control.

Rare, indeed.

Then I got the buzz.

It was a combination of sound and vibration coming from

my cell phone, which I had tossed face down on the center console between the driver and passenger seats. At that moment, my mental bliss was oblivated by the first thought that entered my mind: it could be "the call" that I anticipated receiving any day now.

News of the results of my stereotactic breast biopsy.

How did I suspect "this was it?"

Quite simply, no one ever calls my cell phone. I kept my Michigan number, which has an area code unfamiliar to most Nebraskans. Therefore, the majority of people call our landline to reach me for fear of being charged extra by their cellular provider. (At least that's the excuse that I'm going with!)

I glanced down at the phone's display.

Yup.

It was doctor's office, all right.

I answered the phone, which I usually refrain from doing when driving. I wish I could say that I'm practicing good citizenship, but – truth be told – my primary motivation is my kids. I'm terrified by the thought that they would – someday in life – answer their phones while driving, i.e. "Well, Mom, you did it!" If something happened to them, I couldn't live with myself. I don't want to be a hypocrite either. So I've trained myself to follow the rules even when it seems that no one else can see.

That is, except for now.

Ok, I'm a hypocrite.

I figured that – even if I answered the call now – it would probably lead to one of those I've-got-to-pull-over-to-the-side-of-the-road-to-take-this moments.

I fumbled for the grab then swiped my iPhone screen to accept the call. After a quick hello on my part, I was immediately taken back – but not by the words on the receiving end. Rather, it was the voice that created what felt like a tiny tear in my heart.

My doctor was making this call rather than her nurse. In every routine or otherwise test that I've ever taken, the nurse usually calls to stay that everything was "normal."

Clearly, this call would be anything but.

I asked if she'd mind waiting a minute.

I slowed down and pulled over, placed our 2004 Honda Pilot in "Park," and settled onto the graveled shoulder of the road. The intermittent shakes, created by other vehicles whipping by on my right side, seemed to aptly emphasize the seriousness of the upcoming conversation. In the next brief span of five minutes, the course of my life could quite possibly be altered, along with every one of my family members.

My now slightly-accelerated heartbeat added to the mechanical trembles. No turning back now (like I really had a choice). With an ever-so-subtle quiver in my voice, I thanked the good doctor for waiting... and told her it was ok to go ahead.

The results showed abnormality.

She then proceeded to refer me to a surgeon.

~

By the time that I pulled the Pilot into our driveway, my eyeglasses were spotted with dried tears. But they were tears of relief and joy, splashed with thanksgiving. Yes, you heard me right! My praiseful disposition was simply a natural response to knowing that my Father in Heaven loves me more than I can imagine.[1]

How can I be so sure?

Psalm 119:160, John 17:17, 2 Timothy 3:16 are just a few of the many verses that testify to the Truth of His Word.[2] Yes, the Lord has been sovereignly present for me spiritually, as I have read and meditated on Scripture every morning. Interestingly, He's also been bringing Bible verses, memorized earlier in life and previously in hiding, to the forefront of my mind.[3]

But God doesn't just share His love for me in written words alone. He has also been bodily present – and actively intervening – through His people and other circumstances. Let's call it "Instant Messaging" with a divine twist. And the Father does it uniquely for every one of His children. It's just that some, I believe, are too busy to notice and celebrate it!

I don't ask for visible evidence of the reality of His existence. I don't need it to be secure in my faith. However, because Jesus so intimately knows and loves me, He often blesses me with eyes to see His supernatural power and presence – at just the right time and in a just-for-me kind of way.

How you may ask?

Proof positive can be found in a recap of the past 72 hours.

~

During the initial mammogram... the technologist was unusually and painstakingly thorough, as if she knew something was up. The spot where the suspicious tissue was found? No surprise to God, it was a nearly-out-of-reach area in the uppermost part of my left breast.[4] I've had at least a dozen mammograms in my lifetime. Never have I seen that level of I'm-not-gonna-give-up attitude from a mammogram technologist. In doing so, she victoriously captured those enemy cells on film. If not discovered, they could have – I shudder to think of it – possibly morphed into an all-out bodily assault. A supernatural power miraculously worked in and through the technician, in such a way those abnormal cells were forced from darkness into the light. (Later, my doctor would comment that she'd never seen these kinds of cells discovered so early in a diagnosis.)

In the waiting room after the mammogram... thankfully, I didn't suspect a thing. In fact, I was browsing through one of those do-it-yourself magazines. *Like, who can paint a chair like that! COME ON, PEOPLE!* Other than the slam at my home improvement capabilities, my mind was completely at ease. That's when the door opened. I heard the unexpected words, *"No need for panic, but we need a closer look..."* I followed the technician into the same room for a second round of images. She continued her pursuit of excellence, certainly bolstered by the fact that Jesus is her CEO in that faith-based hospital. I literally kept my eyes fixed on Jesus; His picture graced the wall in the form of Warner Sallman's Head of Christ.[5] Sure, it's true. Hundreds of women have perhaps glanced upon his face, while their breasts were being smooshed. But I have no doubt that – because He knows me so intimately – God provided this visual affirmation of His presence as the perfect touch of "It's gonna be ok, Chris" to give me the strength needed to endure round #2 of x-ray images.[6]

After the second set of images... the mammogram technologist led me into a small room, where Goliath-size images of my breasts spanned the length of the wall. (Yeah, freaky, huh?) She introduced me to the radiologist. The name sounded familiar, but I'd never met him before. After a few minutes, we discovered that he is married to my leader from the first Bible study that I joined when moving to Lincoln seven years ago. This refreshingly surprising connection defused any shock that could have overtaken me, as Dr. B proceeded to share the news not only as a professional, but also a Brother in Christ. He even respectfully asked if he could tell his wife, who I'm certain lifted me up in pray that very night – and would faithfully continue to do so for the next few days (or possibly weeks) to come.

Less than 24 hours later... I returned to the hospital for a stereotactic breast biopsy, which is a procedure to remove a sample of the troubling tissue with a needle for further examination. (Much to my surprise, I was able to schedule this appointment the day following after my mammogram. The hospital staff member responsible for scheduling was taken back by the appointment's timeliness, as well.) The first face that I see? The technologist who performed my mammogram the day before. She was assigned (by the Lord, no doubt!) to assist in the procedure. All goes well – until I faint during another mammogram, which followed the biopsy. But the team at this Christian hospital cared for me so beautifully.

Later that afternoon following the biopsy... Because the fainting episode kept me detained later than originally scheduled, I could see the impossibility of keeping my afternoon gig as traffic cop at my kids' school. I sent out a few texts in hope of finding a parent to cover for me in 30 minutes, no less! This perhaps is the greatest miracle of all, as finding a volunteer (in general, let alone a sub) to stand midstream in a vehicular loop of anxious elementary-school parents at 3:25PM is no small task. Seconds after I sent the text, a Sister in Christ quickly replied, "No problem!" (She had no idea where I was or the reason for my cry of help.) I downed two OJs, Scooters® shake, and bottled water. (Hey, doctor's orders!) The cherry on top of this miracle-filled day? I make it to school on time to pick up my kids without peeing my pants. Plus I am so bloated up with liquids that there's no time for self-pity; all my thoughts are directed towards self-control of the bladder kind.

~

Merriam-Webster dictionary defines the word "truth" as sincerity in action, character, and utterance. As I have stood firm on the Truth of His Word, He has given me eyes to see exactly that: the *sincerity* of Jesus' love for me *in action* through every moment of these strange days, the *character* of the people placed in my path along the way, and *utterances* or encouragement that He purposely placed in my life throughout this past week.

Non-believers may "poo-poo" and attribute my experiences to superficial descriptions like "coincidence" and "luck." These words were obviously coined by skeptics and cynics. I've vowed to never utter these words again, after my eyes were opened to the Truth that nothing is by chance. The God of the Universe is completely in control.

And there's a guaranteed happy ending to all of it.[7]

Oh, sure. There will probably be a few tears in the weeks to come. But I refuse to allow the Enemy to twist my thinking. I choose to simply walk hand-in-hand in faith with Jesus through the newest part of our story. Like earlier today, I believe there will be more tears of joy than otherwise... overflowing from the knowledge that He is ever-present and always guiding me.

> *You will show me the way of life, granting me the joy of your presence and the pleasures of living with you forever.*[8]

So I'll live in each moment – the here and now – enjoying every precious conversation and revelation with the Love of my life. When fear starts to rear its ugly head, Jesus reminds me – regardless of the biopsy's results – it's a win-win situation. Either I remain on Earth and grow old with Him. Or Jesus ushers me into Paradise for a new beginning, new body, and life everlasting. Luck? I think not. It's the greatest reality that exists.

I'm just traveling through this world.

My home is in heaven.

Does it get any better than that?

Not a chance.

1. For this is how God loved the world: He gave his one and only Son, so that everyone who believes in him will not perish but have eternal life. John 3:16 (NLT)

2. The very essence of your words is truth; all your just regulations will stand forever. Psalm 119:160 (NLT) Make them holy by your truth; teach them your word, which is truth. John 17:17 (NLT) All Scripture is inspired by God and is useful to teach us what is true and to make us realize what is wrong in our lives. It corrects us when we are wrong and teaches us to do what is right. 2 Timothy 3:16 (NLT)

3. I will study your commandments and reflect on your ways. I will delight in your decrees and not forget your word. Psalm 119:15-16 (NLT)

4. You saw me before I was born. Every day of my life was recorded in your book. Every moment was laid out before a single day had passed. Psalm 139:16 (NLT)

5. https://www.warnersallman.com/collection/images/head-of-christ/

6. Even when I walk through the darkest valley, I will not be afraid, for you are close beside me. Your rod and your staff protect and comfort me. Psalm 23:4 (NLT)

7. For it is my Father's will that all who see his Son and believe in him should have eternal life. I will raise them up at the last day. John 6:40 (NLT)

8. Psalm 16:11 (NLT)

PROGNOSIS

Best News Ever

Earlier today, Mike and I met with the surgeon and his team to discuss the results of my recent stereotactic breast biopsy. The prognosis was what we anticipated: SURGERY. In other words, let's get those bastards (the cells screaming PRECANCEROUS under the microscope) out of there.

Right now, I am overwhelmed with extreme gratitude for my hubby, who took the entire morning off from work to come alongside and support me in two critical ways.

First, Mike is a bona fide medical jargon interpreter. He earned his Ph.D. from the University of Minnesota Veterinary College. Oddly enough, animal and humans have some commonalities when it comes to physical affliction. For example, once when I was having eye discomfort, Mike suggested using the same topical ointment prescribed by our vet for our ailing Siberian Husky. I was part insulted, part amused. However, later that afternoon after visiting my general practitioner, can you guess the contents of my little white bag when leaving the pharmacy's drive-up window?

Yup, that's right.

I'm tempted to insert an "AR AR" to emphasize the irony of

the owner-canine connection. However, "ARF ARF" seems strangely more appropriate.

But seriously, Mike's extensive knowledge in bacteriology, virology and other "oglogies" too numerous to mention comes in handy when terminology is WA-AA-AYYYY over my Bachelor of Journalism head. Mike brilliantly brings things down to layman's terms, which often leads to a greater sense of peace – not to mention bonus savings in the family budget, thanks to shared human and canine prescriptions.

Of course, I'm just kidding?

Secondly, Mike is a Godly spouse, best friend and soulmate – all rolled up into one. As the Bible states in Ephesians 5:28:

> *... husbands ought to love their wives as they love their own bodies. For a man who loves his wife actually shows love for himself.*

In other words, I believe that Mike considers this surgery as if it were his own. I will henceforth appropriately call it *our* appointment. Mike and I are united in this predicament (not really sure what to call it) regardless of who is going under the knife. How comforting to know that all my interests – physical, emotional and spiritual – are equally important to my husband as they are to me. I am keenly aware that, especially as we may soon be discussing potentially image-alternating surgery, God perfectly choose this man for me.

That's another blessing of this journey.

I have grown to appreciate Mike more than ever before. Since we became Christ followers, Mike's unconditional love brings to life all Scripture that affirms God's truth about His one-man-and-one-woman-for-life plan. Our marriage is second only to God's promise to His people in terms of everlasting faithfulness.[1] I've been finding myself in even greater awe of this never-ever-gonna-leave-ya' love – and totally aware that this level of commitment, whether demonstrated through my hubby or found within Scripture, ultimately comes from the One who defined love in the first place.[2]

Sure, the Bible is full of stories testifying to this Truth. But now, I wasn't just reading about God faithfully trekking along with a group of weary people thousands of years ago, delivering them from fear and lovingly guiding their every move.[3]

This morning, I personally experienced it.

~

First, Mike and I completed paperwork in the surgeon's waiting area. I looked around and thought about how every person in the room was likely in the midst of some kind of trial. My heart was instantly softened with compassion but also gratitude. I silently thanked God for the timely way that He led me here... and how this scene could have been so different without His protection in revealing the pre-cancerous cells in their early stages of growth.

Next, Mike and I were led to the examination room. We met with Dani, the nurse assigned to the basics: temperature, weight and blood pressure. She asked a few questions about what brought me into the office – even though I'm sure most of the physical details of my case were laid out on her clipboard. Perhaps she was simply trying to access my mental condition. She asked me to change into a gown. Open from the front, she explained. Dani exited the room.

Nothing unusual.

Then Angela arrived.

My mind flashed back to my best friend in 6th grade.

I hadn't thought about Angela in ages, but the name rang a soothing bell. Inside, I felt my heart beat with joy: God knew this little sweet touch of familiarity would put my mind even more at ease! I love the reality of Him working even in the smallest details... and thankful for all the moments – like this one in the examination room – when the Holy Spirit gives me eyes to see that Jesus is always right beside me. Angela explained that surgery was the only option at this point in terms of removing the rebellious cells dubbed "abnormal."

After Angela left the room, I was curious what she meant by abnormal. On my phone, I searched my dictionary app and found the following definition:

DIFFERENT FROM WHAT IS NORMAL OR AVERAGE; UNUSUAL ESPECIALLY IN A WAY THAT CAUSES PROBLEMS.

Yup, that sounds about right.

God zoomed my thoughts out from my self-focused lens to a bigger picture. When God made the world, "normal" was unity not only with Him, but also throughout all creation. Normal was a community – humans plus all other species of life – existing together in peace. Normal was understanding His ways were designed with everyone's best interests in mind. Bottom line? This normal was the quintessential paradise! Then temptation to doubt God's perfect ways entered the scene. Selfishness bullied its way to the forefront. Choosing any way other than the Creator's original design? Basically, a similar scenario to the I'm-gonna-do-my-own-thing-even-if-it-hurts cells in my body.

Different from normal.

And definitely causing problems.

Hmm, I started to wonder... and naturally found myself checking out another definition. (Hey, that's the nature of the writing beast!) This time, I searched for "paradise" and found that one of the first descriptions was EDEN.[4] Out of curiosity, I thought I'd check out antonyms or the opposite of paradise. The first word that appeared on the list?

HELL.

In other words?

The quintessential abnormal.

The surgeon walked into the room. He seemed likable enough. Everything that he said jived with our other two earlier visitors, Dani and Angela, except the terminology was a little more advanced. Again, I thanked the Lord for my medical-term savvy hubby Mike... and allowing him the opportunity to be with me at that moment.

After the appointment, I drove home a little dazed from all the technical lingo packed into the past 1½ hour. But I smiled knowing that, once again, Jesus revealed His faithful love and protection: the surgery was scheduled in less than three weeks – and at the best possible time for our family. Remarkably, the surgeon's only available date coincided perfectly with Mike's work schedule, i.e. no business travel.

Again, I found myself in awe of God's timing.[5]

∾

S o that was this morning and this is now. But today isn't just the day of my consultation with the surgeon.

Today is also Good Friday.

The Lord leads me into a skim-through review of all the pages from the Easter devotional that I've been reading for the past month. It's a compilation of sermons from pastors focusing on the life, death and resurrection of Christ with accompanying Scripture, designed to prepare my heart to truly know the meaning of Jesus' sacrificial love for me over 2,000 years ago.

What catches my eye?

I notice a fluorescent blue Post-it note, written just one day into the start of this devotional – before I had any knowledge that precancerous cells were beginning their covert attack. An arrow scribbled on the note points to a commentary from John Piper centered on Luke 9:51 (ESV):

When the days drew near for him to be taken up, he set his face to go to Jerusalem.

I wrote, "I may not suffer like Christ, but I am aware that this world is not the paradise that God intended."

God brought this devotional into my life for such a time as this. When I started reading it, I had no idea that I would be meeting with a surgeon to schedule the removal of a "lollipop-sized" portion of my breast. Once again, the Lord went before me to provide just the perfect Scripture, knowing all that I would be experiencing right now. He knew these readings would be the divine ammunition needed to combat any self-destructive thoughts that I may have been tempted to dwell on during the past few weeks.

Yes, I will emerge a scarred woman after the May 3 surgery. Only God knows how much tissue will be removed. Yes, if the abnormal cells are deemed cancerous, I will move forward into radiation and, potentially, a full mastectomy of one or both breasts. Yes, the end result could be my departure from this Earth a little earlier than I expected.

I understand all those "what if's."

But I refuse to dwell on these possibilities. Because at this point, they are only possibilities! I know where that path of thinking-too-far-ahead leads – and who takes me down that dark road. Hint: It's not Jesus! I find myself asking: *How can I doubt God, especially when He has brought me so lovingly through everything I have experienced so far?*

At this point, Chris Tomlin's song "Whom Shall I Fear" starts swirling in my head.[6]

Last night, I shared God's "Fear not!" wisdom with my 9-year-old daughter Mia, whose eyes quickly teared up when hearing about the surgery. I explained that "what if's" are one of Satan's greatest tools of deception for stealing our joy. Instead of living in the moment, he tries to distract us with a hell of doubt and worry. It's especially in times like last night… when I'm snuggling with my precious girl during tuck-ins… that I am so thankful for God's Word! His Truths not only victoriously slay the Enemy's attacks on my personal sanity, but also enable me to minister to my equally-in-this-situation family. As I've remained committed to hang out with Jesus every morning, He continues to keep me in the Paradise of knowing that His Love is unconditional, unfailing and unending.

Gotta love all those "un's!"

Funny thing?

The Easter devotional that I'm camped out in right now has sat on my shelves for over three years! I always intended to read it. But now I see the Lord was waiting to bless me with it.

Gotta love His perfect timing.

As I have meditated on this devotional over the past weeks, the Lord has revealed the beauty of dwelling on Jesus instead of me. That is, setting my face on Him instead of my circumstances. I realize that nothing my mind or body endures over the next days, months or years could ever compare to Jesus' sacrifice, which was far from only physical. Jesus took on the spiritual wrath of God for *every* sin. Committed by *every* person. *Past, present and future.* No matter what happens to me, I will never suffer like Jesus did. On the cross, He was separated from God – which is the very definition of hell itself – taking the punishment that I deserved. Why? He loved me and wanted me to be with Him in Paradise.[7]

SWEETER   153

Paradise *today* in my earthly trials.

Paradise *forever* with my heavenly Savior.

Thanks to His amazing grace, I've been freely offered (and gladly accepted) FOREVER LOVE that can never be destroyed by surgery or anything else, both in this world and one to come.

And that prognosis?

It's the best news ever.

---

1. But the love of the Lord remains forever with those who fear him. His salvation extends to the children's children of those who are faithful to his covenant, of those who obey his commandments! Psalm 103:17-18 (NLT)
2. Dear friends, let us continue to love one another, for love comes from God. Anyone who loves is a child of God and knows God. But anyone who does not love does not know God, for God is love. 1 John 4:7-8 (NLT)
3. But Moses told the people, "Don't be afraid. Just stand still and watch the Lord rescue you today. The Egyptians you see today will never be seen again. The Lord himself will fight for you. Just stay calm." Exodus 14:13-14 (NLT)
4. Eden is the place where Adam and Eve lived before choosing "abnormal." Check it out in Genesis 2:8–3:24.
5. You go before me and follow me. You place your hand of blessing on my head. Psalm 139:5 (NLT)
6. https://www.youtube.com/watch?v=q24z4XcJxnM
7. God showed how much he loved us by sending his one and only Son into the world so that we might have eternal life through him. This is real love —not that we loved God, but that he loved us and sent his Son as a sacrifice to take away our sins. 1 John 4:9-10 (NLT)

LIVING PROOF

84th & Old Cheney

MASTECTOMY.

I'm tempted to use a scary font to bring this word to life in full force on the page. But you and I know, especially if you're of the female persuasion, elaboration of this medical term is unnecessary.

It's pretty much synonymous with FEAR.

When the word was first uttered in our initial consultation with the surgeon a few days ago, Mike's face was immediately awash with concern. And he's the unshakable, even keel counterpart in this one flesh union! His own feelings aside, Mike seemed to emphatically mourn alongside me for the potential partial loss of a body part that – in our culture – seems to so define womanhood.

Later that evening, despite the fact that I shared the news matter-of-factly, I saw "the look" in my 4th grade daughter Mia's eyes; it seemed to communicate an innate understanding that this procedure has the potential to deeply pierce more than just a woman's physical being. For whatever reason, good or bad, whether maternal instincts or aesthetics, I believe most women would agree that our breasts are one area that no one would like as the focal point of an invasive surgery.

Honestly, my anxiety level has been far below what the "old" Chris would have exhibited – from the first mention of the word "suspicious" at my initial mammogram to the consultation with the surgeon a few days ago. Clearly, Jesus has been actively and lovingly involved throughout this life experience. I've felt His presence especially when alone and my mind wanders... as fearful thoughts of the unknown attempt to chip away my faith. In the battlefield of my mind, I have lifted up everything to the Lord in prayer.

Truly, I've known peace that surpasses all understanding.[1]

At least I *did* know that peace – before I allowed my mind to begin dwelling on two words that the surgeon threw out towards the end of our consultation: partial mastectomy. What did I do in response? Well, of course, I bluntly yelled out "WHAT?!"... tempered afterwards with a request for clarification as respectfully as I could muster while still in shock. He smiled. Then he said it was "simply semantics"... explaining that partial mastectomy was just another term for excisional breast biopsy.

That put my mind at ease.

At least temporarily.

❧

A couple days later, a hospital admissions rep called to talk me through more details about the surgery.

She kept using the "M" word.

That triggered something inside me.

Well, it wasn't exactly a trigger. It was more like a sledgehammer plummeting my head, which – up until that point – was filled with peace and focused on my Savior! After the phone call, with me alone at home with my MacBook Pro, I decided to further investigate.

Big mistake.

I googled.

I thought, how bad could it be?

Based on one glimpse of the first unsettling mid-section only photo on the screen, I began to suspect that this search – and perhaps others similar to it – could likely be undermined in part by the Prince of Darkness. I mean, COME ON!! The problem of Internet porn alone is enough to make one wonder who (or what) has their hooks in this technology. The Enemy of our souls has GOT to be in there somewhere... as hundreds of websites, images, videos and shopping sources bombard you every second... many undoubtedly from questionable sources. The end result is nothing less than mental chaos.

Although it probably wasn't intended to be, Google could arguably be the greatest nemesis of Philippians 4:8-9, which prescribes an iron-clad remedy for living in peace:

Fix your thoughts on what is true, and honorable, and right,
and pure, and lovely, and admirable. Think about things
that are excellent and worthy of praise. Keep putting into
practice all you learned and received from me—everything
you heard from me and saw me doing. Then the God of peace
will be with you.

I left my computer screen with warped images painfully carved in my mind. I mean, WHY DID I EVEN GO THERE!? Before I even clicked the "Return" key, I knew in my heart of hearts that googling was a bad idea. But I did it anyway. I took my eyes off Jesus and redirected them to my computer screen.

The damage was done.

Or was it?

∽

The following morning after the Google fiasco, I experienced a very interesting encounter with Jesus during our Quiet Time together. The next chapter in my devotional was written by Joni Eareckson Tada titled "Crucified with Christ." The topic? Joni and her husband's personal experience when faced with breast cancer and – you guessed it.

Mastectomy.

Double mastectomy, to be precise.

But still, I left my morning Quiet Time feeling strengthened by the Spirit-powered words of this leader in Christian faith.[2] I knew the timing of this devotional couldn't be "coincidental." Quite simply, that's not a viable word in any Christ-follower's vocabulary. However, when I left that peaceful place on my living room floor – and the reassuring voice of Jesus – my weaknesses came out front and center. Moments after entering our bedroom for our daily prayer time, Mike soon had his arms wrapped around me tight... while my eyes began overflowing with tears... erupting into sobbing... with a grand finale of speechlessness.

Fear had overwhelmed me.

∽

Over several days, I tried to convince myself that I didn't care about the partial loss of my left breast. Mike insisted that our prayers be simply focused and twofold: #1 remove all abnormal cells and #2 those cells would be cancer-free. No mention of physical appearance, although – in my heart – I kept wanting to add prayer #3: *Do not take more than is needed!* Surely, I was not superficial enough to put appearance over my health.

Surely?

Mike has assured me that he loves me no matter what my appearance. Even Jesus, divinely intervening, continues to reveal a spiritual and eternal love for me that surpasses all earthly definitions of beauty. But lingering doubts still persisted. All the while, one name kept popping in and out of my psyche.

Sarah.

This name has flickered through my thoughts repeatedly over the past few days. Sarah has been one of the players in my Bunco group for over seven years, as well as the mother of a friend in Mia's class at school. Bunco is a dice game. Once a month, 12 women get together to play a mindless game where winning consists purely by the roll of the dice. It's not the game, however, that makes these get-togethers so appealing.

One Friday night every month, each one of us breaks away from our same-old, same-old responsibilities as mothers, wives and working professionals. We laugh until tears stream from our eyes and exchange thoughts on everything from tips on how to get an adorably stubborn, flip-flop lovin' toddler to don proper footwear in winter or the best books that we've read as of late. Most of these women I only see once a month. That's another aspect that makes every Friday Bunco Night a can't-miss and if-I-don't-go-mamma's-gonna-lose-her-sanity thing. I look forward to every one! These women are genuinely fun and refreshingly authentic. (And unlike my former days, there's not a drop of alcohol in these not just good but oh-so-great times.)[3]

In addition to being a Bunco player, Sarah works as a nurse at St. E's Hospital, where the surgery will be performed one week from today.

I'm friends with many Sisters in Christ who are nurses, including three of our "Bunco Babes." (That's a term of endearment that our 12 players like to toss around, but – believe me! – none of us think that we're "all that.") Also, the number of nurses in the 250+ member Bible study that I enjoyed before moving to the country is too numerous to count!

In our small discussion groups in that Bible study, I heard these amazing ladies share their experiences in the workplace. No names were ever mentioned; they also possess the Godly trait of loyalty. Continually, I thanked God that He placed each one of these women in such a critical – and often timely – position to minister to those patients in their care, both medically and spiritually.

I still don't know why it was Sarah's name alone that kept resurfacing in my thoughts. But I suspected that she probably knew something about this particular surgeon, as they both worked at the same hospital.

Should I ask Sarah?

I don't know how many times I asked my husband that question. But I do know that – at one point – he replied with visible irritation, "JUST PLEASE CALL HER!" It was uttered in a tone, I'm sure, that was love mixed with an underlying need for his own personal sanity.

But I just couldn't do it.

I kept telling myself that my desire to have Sarah confirm or deny any suspicious activity related to the surgeon or his reputation was a sign of doubt. I wanted to ask her point blank: *"He's not known as 'The Butcher,' is he?"* Only if Jesus miraculously crossed our paths would I pose any question to her – although probably not as graphic as my fearful mind would ask it!

If you want me to talk to Sarah, send her my way.

That was the request to my beloved Savior.

Hence, earlier this morning, the One who knows me intimately reached down from Heaven. Lovingly and compassionately, He answered my request, speaking reassuringly to me through a supernatural intervention.

He, the Creator and God of the Universe, didn't have to do it.

But He did.

And in a very physical way.

~

ow's it going, Chris?
I heard a voice behind me, as I exited the school building's front doors – nearly 20 minutes after the first period bell rang. The students were now working at their desks. Any parents who dropped off their little ones should have been long gone.

Yet there she was.

I hate to admit it, but I have no recollection of our first few minutes of chitchat. I wonder what my eyes were communicating to this smiling woman, as I must have looked visibly taken back when Sarah initially greeted me.

Stunned – but in a good way – is more like it.

We walked out of the school together engaged in small talk, eventually reaching the corner where the sidewalk parts. This marked the spot where we would go our separate ways.

So I gave it a shot.

Sarah, I'm not sure if God wants me to share this with you....

That's when I let it all spill out. Not tears, but all the events of the past few weeks, in addition to the anxiety created by Mike and my consultation with the surgeon. Sarah listened carefully and with visible sympathy. She then proceeded to comfort me with three enlightening words which – up to this point – had never entered my mind.

HE'S A MAN!

My eyes opened wide.

The "aha" moment settled in.

She was right.

In addition to his utmost professionalism (which I truly

appreciate), the surgeon was simply presenting a "man's take" on the upcoming procedure. Because of God's distinctive creation of male vs. female, he could *never* communicate the same level of emotion and empathy that I had experienced from all the female medical professionals (i.e. fellow breast possessors) that God had thus far placed in my life.

I don't mean to stereotype. But let's get real. Although male and female are created in His image, both sexes are obviously uniquely designed not just physically but also in disposition.[4]

For example, I appreciated and needed the perfectly timed back massages from my female nurses – both for physical and emotional reasons – during the initial mammogram and follow-up biopsy. A man never could have provided this bodily comfort for legal reasons and otherwise. I was comforted beyond words with their compassionate eyes that clearly communicated, "I get it," not just as RNs but as women.

Men don't have breasts.

NUF SAID.

My anxiety was instantly shattered by not only the "aha" moment, but also a chorus of chuckling between two Sisters in Christ... followed by what I felt was the warmest hug that I've ever experienced. Sarah then put on her nurse's hat and proceeded to assure me that – despite his matter-of-fact approach in the examination room – the surgeon would not remove anything beyond what was necessary.

She affirmed that he was, indeed, an excellent surgeon.

We talked for nearly an hour, not only about the surgery but other faith-building stuff of life. I later found out that Sarah was headed to the grocery store; she was going to make a meal for another friend in crisis.

I was comfort *and* inspired by this amazing Sister in Christ.

Before we parted ways, Sarah wrapped her arms around me

one more time. And something happened for the first time since the surgeon's appointment a few days ago.

I felt no fear.

Of course, I know it was Jesus working through Sarah. He set up our encounter. Then He gave Sarah just the perfect words to assure me of His omnipresence. That's a fancy word for that wonderfully "always present everywhere" quality that can be attributed to no one and nothing else other than the Almighty God and Creator of the Universe.

Why would He do this?

Because Jesus loves and knows me better than anyone! He created me. I believe that – despite my doubts and fears – He continues to pursue me even when my faith in His can't-shake-em-or-break-em promises is swallowed up by an earthly circumstance. Or my human frailty leaves me sadly prone with an inability to believe Him. Quite simply, He'll do whatever it takes to convince me that nothing can separate me from His Love.[5]

Like divinely bringing Sarah into my morning.

You see, I typically don't see Sarah at school. In fact, I don't recall one time since the year began seven months ago that we've crossed paths in the hallway or parking lot. Although Jesus tried, my stubborn fears couldn't be eased, despite all the times that He spoke to me so sweetly over the past week via the Holy Spirit. Therefore, He chose to minister to me, perfectly timed and without condemnation, in very physical way.[6]

Sarah's smile. *His gentle assurance.*
Sarah's words. *His life-giving voice.*
Sarah's hug. *His protective grip.*

No one has ever seen God. But if we love each other, God lives in us – and His Love is brought to full expression in us.[7] That Love was definitely expressed through Sarah!

This world calls it kindness. But we followers of Jesus? We know the Truth. This kindness is the Spirit of God himself living inside of His beloved children. And the Spirit is one of the gifts that God freely gives to anyone who cries out, "I BELIEVE!"[8]

Jesus personified.

This Spirit allows us to enjoy a glimpse of His glorious Kingdom to come... where the "M" word is nowhere to be found. Fear has been erased. And nothing remains but peace and love. As a citizen, along with all of God's holy people, I'll not only see my Savior face-to-face... but also be forever held by the arms of the One who created "hugs" in the first place!

No semantics here.

It's simply living proof.

---

1. Then you will experience God's peace, which exceeds anything we can understand. His peace will guard your hearts and minds as you live in Christ Jesus. Philippians 4:7 (NLT)
2. https://www.joniandfriends.org/about/our-leadership/
3. Don't be drunk with wine, because that will ruin your life. Instead, be filled with the Holy Spirit. Ephesians 5:18 (NLT)
4. So God created human beings in his own image. In the image of God he created them; male and female he created them. Genesis 1:27 (NLT)
5. And I am convinced that nothing can ever separate us from God's love. Neither death nor life, neither angels nor demons, neither our fears for today nor our worries about tomorrow—not even the powers of hell can separate us from God's love. No power in the sky above or in the earth below—indeed, nothing in all creation will ever be able to separate us from the love of God that is revealed in Christ Jesus our Lord. Romans 8:38-39 (NLT)
6. And the King will say, "I tell you the truth, when you did it to one of the least of these my brothers and sisters, you were doing it to me!" Matthew 25:40 (NLT)
7. 1 John 4:12 (NLT)
8. And when you believed in Christ, he identified you as his own by giving you the Holy Spirit, whom he promised long ago. The Spirit is God's guarantee that he will give us the inheritance he promised and that he has purchased us to be his own people. He did this so we would praise and glorify him. Ephesians 1:13-14 (NLT)

SURGICAL PREP

Raising the Bar

It's 4:29AM on Friday, just three hours before I'm scheduled to be admitted for outpatient surgery.

In less than 60 minutes, I need to take off my wedding ring. Then jump in the shower – just me and my skin – to scrub down from head-to-toe with an anti-bacterial soap bar. That clunky white brick, in-and-of-itself, elevates my morning routine to a new level of weirdness. I'm a shower gel gal. But apparently Dial® soap bars are one of the surgical world's go-to's for home pre-surgical cleansing. Before last week, I was unaware of this under-the-knife technicality.

In a few words?

Let the countdown begin.

My head is somewhat swirling with things on the "Do Before Leaving for Hospital" list. Like waking up two tweens 1 1/2 hours earlier than usual... helping them ready for their school amid a mild case of sleep deprivation... and releasing the beasts. (That's Huetherism for feeding and exercising our two Siberian Huskies before throwing them back in their kennels.)

Yet with all the unusualness of this morning, the Lord has led me to my computer keyboard.

I came out here to my Quiet Time space expecting to dive into a new Psalm – one that I thought would be perfectly suited to today's adventure. However, as I was searching Bible Gateway, my iPad screen continued loading the Scripture that God spoke to me yesterday morning.

Psalm 66.

It's about worship.

Not worship defined as singing in church every Sunday. Or spending ½ hour or more daily reading the Bible. (Although that's all good!) Rather, Psalm 66 is telling me that bursting out in spontaneous praise – *every day and all day* – is a can-do and wanna-do! As someone who has personally experienced God's saving grace – *every day and all day* – I'm definitely on board for giving the Lord a shout-out for all His glorious character, awesome deeds, and never-failing responses to this crazy lady's every prayer.

SHOUT JOYFUL PRAISE TO GOD, ALL THE EARTH!

— PSALM 66:1

How refreshing that my thinking is camped out right now in THANKSGIVING versus the flip-side from my non-believing days. (I likely would have been complaining or seeped in bitter-ness.) Once again, I find myself asking the question that enters my mind whenever trials come my way: *How does anyone make it through this life without Jesus?!*

As I type this morning, I wonder if perhaps the Lord doesn't want me to forget how His Love has dramatically changed me through this could-be-cancer story. From that initial mammogram until now, He has revealed with every new chapter that I'm not the same woman that I used to be.

Case in point?

Unlike previous major trials in my life, I no longer want to shut myself away from all society. Although, I must confess, I still didn't answer the phone last night. Mostly, though, for the same reasons as always: Delayed tuck-in equals cranky kids and an unpleasant before-school experience the following morning. No, thank you. Been there, done that. Don't wanna go back! So I told myself long ago: *Let it ring, Sister. Just let it ring.*

Ok, back to this "new creation" thing.

Today, I find myself excited about opportunities to share with others all the God moments that I've been blessed with since the words "suspicious activity" were used to describe those nasty cells inhabiting my left breast. More and more, I'm reflecting on how He's recently moved me outside my comfort zone to follow suit with the psalmist's exuberance:

SING ABOUT THE GLORY OF HIS NAME!

— PSALM 66:2

Ok, maybe not sing.

That would horrify my children and, well, probably most of the civilized world within a 5-mile radius of our home. But you get the picture. Instead, I decide to reflect back on some Holy Spirit-driven moments over the past week. (Hey, it sure beats dwelling on the fact that I'm downright parched and hungry, due to more standard pre-operating procedures, i.e. no food or H2O after midnight prior to surgery day).

Insert stomach growl here.

MONDAY

I took a huge leap of faith by posting an overview of my situation on Facebook®. That may not sound like a big deal. But I can count the number of my previous posts on one hand, since joining this social network megalodon. Ok, maybe two hands, if you consider an occasional "We're having a bonfire this weekend!" on my daughter Mia's Class of 2022 group page. (Ironically, I'm the parent who offered to set up this group and still know virtually zip about the ins-and-outs of Facebook!)

I have nothing against fellow Sisters in Christ sharing personal snippets via social media. I definitely enjoy all the photos! Many are posted by friends that I may never see in person again, due to relocations and other life changes. I'm just still wrestling with how to use Facebook in the context of God's Kingdom. My kids always chuckle, *"Mom, you don't have to end everything with 'Praise the Lord'!"*

I prayed and sensed the Lord was saying "ok" to a post on Facebook. I then asked Him to give me the words, so the focus would be asking for prayers versus soliciting sympathy. And of course, I invited others to join the Huether's in praising God for all the blessings already miraculously provided for our family! Two minutes after the post, I heard a "bleep." Then another. And another. Like fireworks personally delivered from God's heavenly artillery, it was one of the most spectacular shows of the Body of Christ that I've experienced. One by one, friends shot out their expressions of love with commitments to pray for me and my family.

I was surprised.

Overwhelmed.

And humbled.

I also realized how my hesitation toward social media had prevented me from seeing how God can work anything together for the good of those who love Him.[1] I witnessed the power of prayer brought to the forefront for all to see, including not only Sisters in Christ but also non-believing friends and relatives. My post on Monday showed me that it's ok to be real – and go out on a social limb. That is, as long as my Savior is holding onto the branch!

In the end, I knew that the post wasn't just about a surgery.

It was about God's glory.

TUESDAY

I was still marveling in the outpouring of support from friends via Facebook, when I received an email from one of my dearest Sisters in Christ. But the words inside were not what I expected. One thing that surprised me about all the Facebook replies from my initial post is that no one – up to this point – typed the words, "I'm sorry." I've never realized the impact of these two words, until they appeared on my computer screen. I know that my friend meant no harm.

But it just didn't feel right.

In the midst of my personal storm, I liken it to a 50 mph wind gust that attempts to knock you off your feet… just when you thought that you were finally standing solidly on the Rock. You're reciting Scripture. Listening to uplifting Christian music. Focusing your thoughts on NOW vs. the dreaded "WHAT IF's. Then BOOM!

"I'm sorry."

You're sideswiped with a bout of doubt.

At least that's how it seemed to me.

Think about it.

God is aware of everything that will happen in your life.[2] There are no surprises to Him. He knows and loves you more intimately than anyone.[3] And the Lord says that He has great plans for His people.[4] Now I'm not proposing being unsympathetic towards others who are experiencing pain or suffering. But don't those two words seem to kind of imply that maybe THERE ISN'T A PLAN... GOD DIDN'T KNOW... or perhaps He's not so good after all... or – GASP – HE DOESN'T REALLY LOVE ME? Bottom line: Those two words created an uncomfortable temptation to shake off my God confidence. And I'm not going there.

My vote?

Moving forward, I'm choosing to throw "I'm sorry" out of my Believer's vocabulary, like "chance" or "coincidence." I think I'll replace it with "How can I pray for you?"

Or maybe just a hug.[5]

WEDNESDAY

I'm on a "God roll," so to speak, the more that I allow Him to work in and through me to glorify His name. The nurse from the hospital calls to find out how I'm doing. (In other words, she's wondering if I'm freaking out, as the date of the surgery is just two days out.) My response? Words of gratitude spill over into my cell phone, as I can't seem to help but share all the "God moments" that I've experienced so far.[6] That is, until I discover that I've been on hold for 23 minutes.

THURSDAY

God called me to "sub" for another mom for traffic duty after school, the day before my surgery no less. When I said, "Yes," I knew that I'd be out there – up front and center – near the entrance of the Elementary building, for all who know to see.

I imagined a few moms may ponder "How is she doing?" as their kiddos jumped in their vehicles. Or maybe a few would wonder if I was cracking under pressure. (Any cracking happened long ago, my friends, and unfortunately not due to surgical reasons but natural wackiness.)

Yes, the world's perspective of a woman about to undergo potentially breast-altering surgery may be more pity than prayer. Yet, there I stood in the student pickup loop, in the Lord's strength. Joyfully waving traffic through... preventing those kids from dashing down the crosswalk... and smiling at those friends of mine who are more "in the know." A couple of ladies stop to say that they're praying. My response: *Thank you!*

I feel good.

~

As I wrap up my reflections of the past week, Jesus is teaching me that worship isn't a moment in time. It's a continuous celebration of knowing that He's in control and loves me. It's an outpouring of gratitude for the One who created me... knows me intimately... and promises to never leave my side.[7] And it's the supernatural joy and peace – the kind that I'm experiencing right now – of knowing I'm going to be ok... no what happens today or during the weeks to come.

So thank you, Psalm 66.

You've shown me that Jesus has given me a reason to live – the countless blessings that I enjoy every day on this Earth, including those precious people that I celebrate as family. But He's also given me a reason to die – the sure hope of spending eternity with the Greatest Love of my life.

So hand me that bar of soap.

I'll raise it high and...

TELL THE WORLD HOW GLORIOUS HE IS![8]

1. And we know that God causes everything to work together for the good of those who love God and are called according to his purpose for them. Romans 8:28 (NLT)

2. Praise the name of God forever and ever, for he has all wisdom and power. He controls the course of world events; he removes kings and sets up other kings. He gives wisdom to the wise and knowledge to the scholars. He reveals deep and mysterious things and knows what lies hidden in darkness, though he is surrounded by light. Daniel 2:20-22 (NLT)

3. I have loved you, my people, with an everlasting love. With unfailing love I have drawn you to myself. Jeremiah 31:3 (NLT)

4. For I know the plans I have for you," says the Lord. "They are plans for good and not for disaster, to give you a future and a hope." Jeremiah 29:11 (NLT)

5. He comforts us in all our troubles so that we can comfort others. When they are troubled, we will be able to give them the same comfort God has given us. 2 Corinthians 1:4 (NLT)

6. Come and listen, all you who fear God, and I will tell you what he did for me. Psalm 66:16 (NLT)

7. Oh yes, you shaped me first inside, then out; you formed me in my mother's womb. I thank you, High God—you're breathtaking! Body and soul, I am marvelously made! I worship in adoration—what a creation! You know me inside and out, you know every bone in my body; You know exactly how I was made, bit by bit, how I was sculpted from nothing into something. Like an open book, you watched me grow from conception to birth; all the stages of my life were spread out before you. The days of my life all prepared before I'd even lived one day. Psalm 139:14-16 (MSG)

8. Psalm 66:2 (NLT)

PITY PARTY

The Graceful Exit

This morning, I don't feel very attractive.

I have a scar on my left breast from Friday's surgery, although I'm definitely not complaining. The procedure was labeled a partial mastectomy, but the visual aftermath was so far from what I anticipated.

When I dared to sneak-a-peak at the incision site, I expected to see – best case scenario – a gaping indentation the size of a Tootsie Pop®, which was the visual description (or should I say forewarning) that the surgeon shared with me and Mike during our initial consultation. However, I am praising God today that His vision for my breast overruled the earthly surgeon. For reasons I will never understand, the Lord enabled the successful removal of all abnormal cells, while leaving only a 1½-inch blood-red scar. At least that's all that I can see through the semi-transparent bandages temporarily adhered to the incision site.

However, the scar isn't why I'm not feeling so good about myself right now. Actually, I'm rejoicing in the fact that a scar is all that remains – and that, basically, everything previously there seems to have remained relatively intact.

So what's got me in this funk?

From the looks of things, I may have neglected to hear a few of the could-possibly-happen details in the post-surgery overview. Much of my body's left side has taken a physical dive into the pool of *"Whoa, what happened here?!"* My leg is covered with an itchy, red rash. A metropolis of igloo-like blemishes has taken up residence on my inner thigh, and I'm not fond of these irritating new inhabitants. The third finger of my left hand, which usually totes my single-band wedding ring, is monstrously swollen. I was required to remove my ring prior to surgery, and now that stubborn appendage refuses to slip back into its 25-year-old bridal attire.

The tip of my pity party iceberg?

Of course, it would be something seemingly insignificant – and admittedly embarassingly – for a woman who successfully emerged from surgery relatively unscathed to even bring up. (But – Hey! – I'm human.)

A mountain-sized zit is peaking near my upper lip. On the morning of the surgery, I woke up to find this blistering companion. This unanticipated addition to my already vulnerable mental state was not welcomed. I was required to enter the hospital wearing no lotions or cosmetics; however, this bad boy is so big, it would have been wasted effort to even try any camo, i.e. concealer caked on to the max. And, wouldn't you know it, I actually *did* see someone I knew when I woke up from surgery; she happened to be walking by my hospital room and stopped to see what was up (besides the facial volcano visibly erupting above my half-hearted smile).

Can you tell this bothers me?

ARRGH!!

So I'm feeling like a loser, both inside and out.

Apparently, today, I've taken up a leadership role in Vanity Central. And since I'm somewhat physically incapacitated, so I can't even sit down on the proverbial throne.

Seriously, though, this is not a good place to be.

Plus the Devil is screaming in my brain, "WHAT ABOUT THE STARVING CHILDREN?!!" Yes, I am well aware that my situation right now ranks far down on the hardships of the world scale, thank you.

I can't help the way that I feel.

But that's not the worst of it.

During this morning's Quiet Time with Jesus, I'm finding myself not only physically out of whack but also mentally distracted. I'm struggling with being fully engaged in conversation and listening to my Savior, who has been the sole reason for my mental composure over the last 30 days. No matter how hard I try, my thoughts drift off into menial tasks of the day.

Basically, that darn To-Do List is head-butting me again. Apparently, my propensity to be driven by performance is so intense, not even invasive surgery can stop its merciless engine!

It makes me sick that I can't seem to concentrate on Him.

Pathetic is more like it.

As of late, I've been committed to reading through the entire Book of Psalms, from start to finish. I read and reflect on one each morning. Today landed me on Psalm 69:

> *O God, you know how foolish I am;*
> *my sins cannot be hidden from you (v. 5).*

While I'm reading through it, I'm trying so hard to remain focused. But I feel so ashamed right now – so immersed in self pity – it's hard to believe that He would want to be with me! On the floor, I'm resting on my elbows and knees – my usual stance when reading Scripture. I set aside my Bible. Curl up with my forehead touching the carpet. Rest my eyes closed.

And wait.

～

I'm not sure how much time went by... but I found my mind drifting away from my cozy spot on the living room rug and into a vision...

... *I'm on my knees in the courts of the King....*

... *face down before His throne...*

... *trembling in fear.*

In this mental imagery, I am keenly aware of my inferiority in contrast to His majesty. While I'm definitely physically out of it – sore from surgery and still fatigued – my consciousness starts taking me down an even more debilitating path. It's ridden with shame and guilt... as I begin to reflect on the ugliness that I know that I'm capable of deep within my thought life. I find myself immersed in the harsh reality of two totally contrasting images: Selfish me and the Holy of Holies.

I cannot lift my eyes to look at Him. I'm speechless. Unworthy beyond words. Yet how does He greet me? Shockingly, I do not receive what I expect from the King of Kings. It's certainly not what I deserve.

He softly calls me by name.

He gently reaches out His hand...

He kindly summons me closer...

He lovingly invites me to rest at His feet.[1]

He then reaches down... cradles my tear-drenched cheeks tenderly in His hands.... gazing at me right in the eyes with a look of friend who longs to be reunited. No condemnation. Not a trace of my ugly remains in His presence.[2] All that remains is beauty itself.

That would be Jesus.

He blesses me with a new perspective – first, in respect to my physical scars and blemishes. This appearance-obsessed world may see them as imperfections. Jesus and I, however, know that each one marks a chapter in my redemption story.

Take my surgery scar, for example. As a child of the King, I know this deep crimson stripe is a definitive mark of God's divine intervention. If the pathology report reveals cancer, I will praise Him for the early diagnosis. If I am deemed cancer-free, I will praise Jesus for His protection. In either case, this scar is a LOVING REMINDER that my life is always safe in His omnipotent hands.

How about the silvery-white ripples near my abs, which once stood out as the perfect six-pack in our local gym? Stretch marks are rarely valued in a superficial culture toting tummy tucks and liposuction. But after years of amenorrhea and wondering if pregnancy was even a possibility, I consider these marks of childbirth to be a GLORIOUS TESTIMONY of two of the greatest gifts that God has given me – Chase and Mia.[3]

I also begin to reflect on scars that marked my life before becoming a Christ follower. I sense Jesus wondrously transforming my thinking about those moments, too.

For example, I have a noticeable mini-crater, opposite of my elbow, in the bendable part of my right arm. This needle mark represents hundreds of hours in a hospital-like recliner, when I donated plasma in college to help pay for tuition and supplies. Twice a week, I would sneak out of my sorority downtown to the plasma center, fearful that someone would see me. Today, the deep depression in my skin no longer signifies shame and hopelessness. It's now a PRECIOUS REMEMBRANCE that God never gives up... doesn't wish for anyone to choose hell... and actively pursues sinners like me.[4]

Finally, there's the scar engraved on my heart – and Chase's left temple just above his eye – which serves as evidence of God's AMAZING GRACE. When my son was three year old, I left him alone in a moment of frustration – just long enough for him to crawl into an indoor kennel and pull on our dog's ear for attention. God saved my son from losing his vision. But He turned my bad into good, as I took the first step toward acknowledging my need for a Savior.[5] Shortly thereafter, I became the first one in our family to say "Yes!" to His free gift of salvation. Through my conversion, Jesus sparked a whole new first generation of Believers, as my husband and children soon followed.

Let me make it perfectly clear: Jesus didn't cause these scars. Each one was brought about by the poor choices of a sinful woman (that would be moi) or the circumstances of living in a corrupted world – one that's far from the Garden of Eden that God originally created for his people.

Webster's dictionary defines scar as "a mark left on the skin where a wound has not healed completely." That's the world's definition. But the Bible says that Christ appeared after His resurrection with His hands and side still visibly pierced – and offering eternal life for all who believed. The disciples were filled with joy! Perhaps the word "scar" in the KINGDOM dictionary has a greater meaning beyond what human eyes can see. Perhaps our *earthly uglies* turn into His SPIRITUAL LOVELY... when we align ourselves with His Holy Spirit:

Trials bring TRUST.

Worries transform into PEACE.

Mistakes testify to His GRACE.

Problems become PRAYERS.

Earthly death is conquered by ETERNAL LIFE.

Cold religion is replaced by RELATIONSHIP.

As I hammer out His revelations to me on the computer keyboard right now, I don't yet know the end of this possibly-cancer season of my life. I do know, however, that a double mastectomy could be one scenario, depending on the pathology results, as mentioned by the surgeon in our initial consultation. So what if that possibility becomes reality?

My weakness becomes HIS STRENGTH.[6]

Why? I believe in the God that's been redeeming lives, transforming wrongs into right, for over 2,000 years. Regardless of how I look or feel – or what others may think – my Savior has promised to stick with me, now and for all eternity.[7] That's not wishful thinking. It's undeniable proof of His Love.

> *The humble will see their God at work and be glad. Let all*
> *who seek God's help be encouraged. (v. 32)*

Despite all my imperfections. Never mind my distractions. Not because of who I am or what I've done. Rather, it's because of who HE is... and what HE did for me on the cross.[8]

As of right now, I'm officially exiting the woe-is-me party. Putting away streams of guilt. Ripping down signs of regret. I'm walking out the door... knowing that God's not-of-this-world love for me is definitely cause for real celebration.

SO PARTY ON, Sisters!

Not with pity, but with the Truth that you're loved.

Unconditionally.

Scars and all.

---

1. One thing I ask of the LORD – the thing I seek most – is to live in the house of the Lord all the days of my life, delighting in the LORD'S perfections and meditating in his Temple. Psalm 27:4 (NLT)
2. Therefore, since we have been made right in God's sight by faith, we have peace with God because of what Jesus Christ our Lord has done for us. Because of our faith, Christ has brought us into this place of undeserved privilege where we now stand, and we confidently and joyfully look forward to sharing God's glory. Romans 5:1-2 (NLT)
3. Children are a gift from the Lord; they are a reward from him. Psalm 127:3 (NLT)
4. The Lord isn't really being slow about his promise, as some people think. No, he is being patient for your sake. He does not want anyone to be destroyed, but wants everyone to repent. 2 Peter 3:9 (NLT)

5. Come close to God, and God will come close to you. Wash your hands, you sinners; purify your hearts, for your loyalty is divided between God and the world. James 4:8 (NLT)

6. Each time the Lord said, "My grace is all you need. My power works best in weakness." So now I am glad to boast about my weaknesses, so that the power of Christ can work through me. 2 Corinthians 12:9 (NLT)

7. How precious are your thoughts about me, O God. They cannot be numbered! I can't even count them; they outnumber the grains of sand! And when I wake up, you are still with me! Psalm 139:18-19 (NLT)

8. He personally carried our sins in his body on the cross so that we can be dead to sin and live for what is right. By his wounds you are healed. 1 Peter 2:24 (NLT)

PICTURE PERFECT

No Greater Love

I glanced at my cell phone and noticed that I missed a call. The number looked somewhat familiar.

I pondered whether or not to check my voice mail at that moment... or hammer a few things off my To-Do List. Without even thinking, my fingers seemed to find their way to the "Listen to Voice Mail" section of my iPhone.

It was Dani from the surgeon's office.

She asked me to call her back.

Immediately, I returned her call. The receptionist informed me that Dani was going to be hard to reach, because she was visiting with patients most of the day. However, she would forward my message to her.

When I'm expecting an important call – and can't afford to miss it – I don't want to be fully engaged in some time-intensive activity that requires massive thought. Like balancing the checkbook. Or writing a book. Basically, I want to be busied in mind-numbing tasks. Like shredding outdated family financial documents that I've allowed to pile up since 2013. Or scooping turds out of the kitty litter box.

That way, an interruption will be fully embraced as an

escape from the mundane. Plus I can more easily shift my mental gears to be more fully focus on the phone call.

Make sense?

Probably not.

Welcome to my world.

I headed outside to pull weeds.

As I thrusted and wiggled my weed puller deep into the ground, I thanked the Lord for the dozens of dandelions dotting our slightly-dehydrated grass with fuzzy bursts of bright yellow. Thirty minutes seemed to fly under the warm, sunny skies of God's country, as Jesus seemed to have thoughtfully ordered up a perfect 60-degree breeze just for me. It was definitely doing the job to melt away any possible anxiousness.

However, I did find myself glancing down at my cell phone, just to check and – sure enough – I missed a second call from Dani. Darn that ringer! It seems to randomly dictate when I'm available to communicate with the outside world. My phone often remains silent during incoming calls when – I swear! – I thought that I had turned up the volume.

Dani and I were now officially playing phone tag.

This cliché is often associated with frustration. However, I found myself instead positively on fire with determination: I AM GOING TO GET THIS CALL! At that point, I had assigned myself a mission that trumped weeds, laundry and cleaning for Mia's upcoming 10th birthday sleepover.

I was resolute, but not scared. My husband Mike and I were told by the surgeon that 5-7 days was the earliest time frame that the pathology results would be available. (It was only day 4.) I figured that Dani was probably just following up on my post-surgery recovery.

But I still felt compelled to talk with her.

I returned the call, reached the receptionist again, and provided her with our landline vs. my cell phone. *(Take THAT, you darn ringer!)* I quickly ditched the garden tools – no time to stow them away in their proper places in our garage. I knew that I would regret that brief moment of insanity later. Because at least at our house, if Mom lets her guard down EVEN ONCE in terms of putting away items WHERE THEY BELONG immediately after use, it seems like everyone else promptly follows suit.

There's no rest for the rule stickler, that's for sure!

I headed back into the house.

What to do... what to do... what to do...

Without even glancing at my To-Do List, my body seemed to switch into autopilot. In zombie-like style, I meandered into what our family calls the "Creation Station." This small den off to the side of our living room is jam-packed with craft and business supplies. I sat down at my MacBook alongside its sidekick printer. For some reason, my choice of productively-pass-some time-away-while-waiting activity seemed to choose itself.

I began printing out family photos.

In our house, we have a bulletin board adjacent to our entryway. A verse of Scripture ablaze in gold and black calligraphy above the board reads:

Rejoice in the Lord ALWAYS.
Philippians 4:4

When we moved here about a year ago, this bulletin board was one of the first items to grace our new walls. My intent was, every so often, to fill it with photos of recent events in our family's life. It would serve as a gentle reminder (especially in times of brother-sister crisis) of all the times God has so richly blessed us – the fun, fellowship, laughter and smiles.

I had been pretty faithful to the task, that is, until we returned from our one-week family vacation to Mexico in early March. For the past 1 1/2 months, I felt like I'd been running in a feverishly, no-fun "catch up" mode. Hence, the board remained stuck on December with snowball fights and Christmas cheer.

Now the end of the school year was just three weeks away.

Yikes.

Where would I begin?

I scrolled, selected and printed PHOTO AFTER PHOTO AFTER PHOTO from the past few months... sending the printer into a full-color frenzy. Just as quickly as the photos were spitting from the paper tray, my mind was overwhelmed with BLAST AFTER BLAST AFTER BLAST of comforting memories. In other words, THANKSGIVING spilled over into both my mind and my heart. *Wow, we've had a lot of fun over the past two months,* I said to myself.

I guess we really do kinda like each other.

- Our first family adventure to a foreign country
- Mia's final basketball practice and awards ceremony, honoring Coach Dad and every player
- Our Valentine's Day festivities, where love notes to Chase and Mia were scattered throughout the house
- Mia's 4th grade portrayal of Amy Carmichael in the elementary wax museum
- Chase's spaz attack (my 13-year-old is king of interesting facial gestures) when gifted with an iPod
- Mom-daughter trip to "The Musical Adventures of Flat Stanley" at the local community theater
- Chase's massively cracked drum cymbal, official evidence of his entry into the world of hard rock
- Our young musician lugging his equipment outside to worship aloud under God's beautiful blue sky
- Mia's creations from her weekly art class with Mrs. S., an amazing Christian role model at her school
- Mia's crafty shoes made entirely of leopard duct tape

- Unwound toilet paper streaming from a bathroom, courtesy of our irritating but lovable Husky, Redd
- Quails dancing in our flower beds
- Chase stretched out on our ATV, lounging around after our family labored together to build a fire pit
- Mia's 4th grade play and "I can't make it cuz of business travel" Dad surprising her in the audience
- Chase's drum mentor performing in concert
- Our family volunteering at a local faith-based camp to prepare the landscaping for summer

As piles of photos mounted up on the desk in front of me, my gratitude meter was bursting off the charts. These images didn't just represent treasured moments. Each one was a gift from the Creator of the Universe to a group of sinners and misfits. Yup, I'm talking Huethers here. Gotta be honest, we be messy people! But the crazy-cool thing? Even though we don't deserve it, the Lord keeps blessing us with these amazing times and – most importantly – precious relationships for one reason:

His Unfailing Love.[1]

My cell phone rang.

I quickly grabbed it knowing, four rings, and you're out.

Hello?

Yes, it was Dani.

But it wasn't a routine follow-up. Instead, her voice never sounded so sweet, as she spoke the following three words:

You're cancer free.

Tears started to flow. Followed by many questions on my end: *Where did the abnormal cells come from? Will they show up again?* Dani replied that my questions would have to wait until next week. That's when Mike and I were scheduled to meet with the medical team for a post-surgery appointment.

Let the celebration begin.

Of course, I called my hubby immediately. I was tempted to send an email with CANCER-FREE typed in a 200+ font size. But my "I can't wait to tell him!!" phone call was typical of the impulsive enthusiasm that I exhibit with all good news. For a moment, my mind rewinds to years ago... when I saw the positive results on my home pregnancy test... and learned that Mike and I would be blessed with our first child. I stepped out of the bathroom, fully intending to surprise Mike later with one of those "Fun and Creative Ways to Tell Your Spouse that You're Pregnant!" plans. Instead, I blurted out an unrehearsed on-the-spot baby announcement with absolutely no restraint.

Who needs restraint anyway?

BORING!!

That's another plus to hanging out with the Creator daily. He made me this way! In other words, if He loves us, why can't we love ourselves... whether it's a personality quirk – like being overly animated (that I'm probably gonna have forever)... or one of many Jesus-like traits that He'll continue working on developing in me throughout my life via the Holy Spirit.

Is this God amazing, or what!?!

My giddiness and smiles alternated with tears of joy. I also experienced profound silence in awe of my Savior. Sadly, though, my happiness was soon tempered by a reminder of something I learned earlier this week: One of my past co-workers was diagnosed with cancer four years ago. After seeing my Facebook post, she shared encouraging words inspired by her first-hand experience. At the end of her message, she said that she was headed over to a friend's house.

Her friend had just undergone a double mastectomy.

As I recalled other women and their stories brought to light recently... and reflected on how we are all in this together... my emotional state was sobered by the painful reality that – at least while God's people live in this not-what-

He-originally-intended place – there's really is no such thing as cancer-free.[2]

No, this is not a perfect world.

I returned to my bulletin board.

As I pulled off the old photos, the jagged edges of twisted staples threatened me with a bloody poke or two – a reminder that... before and after many of these Kodak® moments... there were undoubtedly a few family conflicts behind the scenes. Perhaps some cross words were regrettably shared later that day. Hurt feelings. Resentment. Complaining. The stuff of life that is definitely not Facebook worthy according to society's standards.

No, this is not a perfect family.

But there is a Perfect Love.

And I can see Him captured in these photos. These picture-perfect snapshots of time capture people who are loving on each other – like He loves on us – if even just for a moment.[3] I thank the Lord for the Holy Spirit, which is not only helping me grow more like Jesus daily, but also every member of this family.

Ironic, isn't it, that the Lord would have me immersed in joyful memories, while awaiting news of a potentially life-altering moment? Interestingly, I did not think about the possibility of cancer once while looking at the photos.

More than ever, I don't ever want to take life for granted.

But of all the blessings, one of the greatest that I've discovered is a new way to worship: the computer keyboard. Four months ago, the Lord mysteriously led me to return to one of my first loves: writing. Little did I know that He would be providing me with more than enough material to fill an entire book – and with unexpected subject matter, including my own cancer scare brought about by anything but a "routine" mammogram.

I am grateful!

And yet, I must confess: At this moment, I feel like beating my dog Redd senselessly for repeatedly head-butting my leg. As

I attempt to type up the final touches on this chapter, he's now graduated to a full-body thrust on my left side. Of course, it's the one that was just subjected to a painful surgery. Gimme some of that Jesus love, please!!

Rejoice in the Lord?

Always.[4]

---

1. Did you know that unfailing love is the most frequent descriptor of God's character in the Old Testament? Source: Commentary on Exodus 15:13 featured in the Filament NLT Print+Digital Bible. Check it out! https://www.tyndale.com/p/filament-bible-nlt/9781496436313
2. But we are looking forward to the new heavens and new earth he has promised, a world filled with God's righteousness. 2 Peter 3:13 (NLT)
3. Jesus said, "So now I am giving you a new commandment: Love each other. Just as I have loved you, you should love each other." John 13:34 (NLT)
4. We also pray that you will be strengthened with all his glorious power so you will have all the endurance and patience you need. May you be filled with joy, always thanking the Father. He has enabled you to share in the inheritance that belongs to his people, who live in the light. For he has rescued us from the kingdom of darkness and transferred us into the Kingdom of his dear Son, who purchased our freedom and forgave our sins. Colossians 1:11-14 (NLT)

UNSHAKABLE

"Mom, Where Are You?!"

4 AM. Yup, that's right.

That's when I start my Quiet Time with Jesus.

Women have asked me when I do my daily Bible study. Doing and studying aren't words that I would use to describe my time with Jesus. It just seems kinda cold. Mundane. Lifeless.

My take?

I am simply enjoying a little sit-down with the Creator of the Universe. Some one-on-one with my all-powerful Savior who once walked on the same planet that I'm living on now. A much-needed time out with the Wonderful Counselor, who keeps me going when times get rough.[1] And a refreshing date in the midst of this crazy world with the Prince of Peace who offers the only slam-dunk guarantee to love me forever.

His name is Jesus.

I've disclosed the time of my daily awakening only a handful of times to friends. The usual response? A wide-eyed glare with one brow noticeably crinkled. Then typically, these two words are blurted out, although not intentionally to hurt my feelings:

YOU'RE CRAZY!

I don't say anything in response. I'm not sure why. It's

certainly not from embarrassment or shame about my faith.[2] Perhaps I don't feel the need to reply because the reality is:

I AM CRAZY!!

Crazy to know and love Jesus more, that is.

After my follow-up appointment with the surgeon yesterday, I've never been so convinced that my unshakable vow to hang out with Jesus daily is the *only* reason that I emerged victorious through this 1 1/2 month "Is it cancer?" rollercoaster ride. God's Word helped me persevere through the emotional tugs-and-pulls of the suspicious mammogram results... initial biopsy with more-than-usual bleeding and a fainting spell... and a ½ day in the Short Stay wing of our local hospital and operating table for what was deemed to be a partial mastectomy.

No doubt, every uncomfortable squish, poke and incision was a bona fide assault on my physical and emotional well-being. Worse of all, I am certain a spiritual assault was taking place, as the Enemy of every man and woman's soul attempted to weaken my resolve to trust in the Lord.[3]

My commitment to not miss a single day of my Quiet Time helped me through one of the "biggies" of my faith tests. Even before I trusted Jesus as my Savior or heard His voice speak to me personally through Scripture, I vowed to do everything humanly possible not to miss our morning coffee dates. Our get-togethers also help me every day with the little trials, too.

Of course, sometimes, I do oversleep. And once in a while, circumstances make it challenging to keep my Jesus rendezvous. Like when our family travels and stays in the same hotel room. Even then, I often go to extremes to keep my morning Loving-on-the-Lord routine. In the wee hours of those vacation mornings, I ever-so-quietly grab the clip-on LED book light and my Bible, which I strategically place on the bedstand the night before. Slide stealth-like down the side of the queen-size bed that I share with my daughter Mia, while peeking over at slumbering Dad and son Chase in our double occupancy room. Covertly land on the frigid industrial-grade carpet. Then gasp at the thought of what nastiness may be lurking there, inconspicuously left behind by previous hotel guests.

Or perhaps their pets.

Gulp.

Initially, when I first began attending church, I would have used "doing" and "studying" to describe my time in God's Word. Truly, I am thankful beyond words for the organized women's Bible studies that welcomed this newbie so graciously into their circles! But in those days, I definitely remember saying that I was afraid of what would happen if I didn't read the Bible daily.

No, I didn't think that God was going to "whack" me.

Rather, my fearful comment reeked of a woman who was relying on her SELF instead of her SAVIOR to handle sibling breakfast battles before school... overcome the stress of being the family's money manager (truly frightening for someone who could barely pass math in her youth)... and – about three years into my faith walk – serving as a small group leader for a Bible study with 16 women *way* more spiritually grounded than me.

I dreaded missing one single morning of completing the 10+ pages on my Bible study sheet. I now know that dread reflected a lack of trust in the Holy Spirit to do what I deemed impossible at that time – stopping outbursts of anger, negative thoughts and words, selfish coveting of my time, and the ugly defense mechanism called sarcasm. *("I was only teasing!")* That was life with Chris at the helm instead of Christ.

I am so glad that those days are long gone.

Oh, I still have my moments! Don't get me wrong. But clearly, the Lord rescued me over the past few weeks from self-pity, worry and doubt – and blessed me with countless opportunities to joyfully testify about how He demonstrated proof of His Love during the could-be-cancer experience. From the time years ago when I first became curious about this God thing, I've tried to immerse myself in His Word.

Even when I didn't feel like it.

Or obstacles seemed to get in the way.

I chuckle recalling the never-ending shifts of AM Quiet Time location, based on my season of life.

Not long ago, you could find me in the master bedroom closet – the only uninterrupted sanctuary that this mama could find living with two early elementary-aged children. On the other side of the door, I could hear the muffled cries, "*WHERE IS MOM!?*" as my husband Mike dutifully served as a heavenly blockade in concealing my hiding place.

After the kiddos' inevitable success in finding me, I relocated with coffee cup, pencil and Bible in hand to the lower level of our home then out the back door to the exterior deck (clad in winter coat in chilly temps). After that, I was forced to venture into the perpetually reckless playroom – prostrated in a playful spiritual formation surrounded by Polly Pocket®, Barbie®, and a few Lego® Friends. I continued to remain on the move, as needed, for spiritual revival.

Fortunately, my mobile manna-fest never made its way to the cold, stony-floored wilderness of our garage or utility room. But if push came to shove, I would have hunkered down by the furnace or lawn mower. I don't, however, think the small engine motor oil for our Craftsman® push-behind mower is what the Lord meant by anointing oil.[4]

Other Scripture immersion techniques?

I changed the setting on our car radio to the Christian station as our family's preferred source of music. *("Wow, Mom, did you realize that every song on the radio is about God?" That was the remark from my then 1ˢᵗ grader one day while driving home from school. Mom smiles.)* The reason was not to shield me or the kids from naughty words or bad lyrics. Rather, after 43 years of music drenched in themes of hopelessness and self-centeredness, I longed for songs that provided more of a positive outlook.[5]

I started memorizing Scripture, tapping into resources like the Navigator's Topical Memory System®.[6] I also sought out Scripture memory songs like Forever Grateful Music's "Hide the Word" series and God Rocks![7] As a family, we realized the benefits of Scripture jam sessions in our Honda Pilot; Chase and Mia's memory verses at their faith-based school were often the very ones played out so beautifully on many of our CDs. Bottom line? At an early age, my kids could not only recall the precious Word of God.

They could also sing it.[8]

I suppose some legalism was unconsciously mixed into *my* early efforts (note the emphasis on "my" efforts rather than in His all-sufficient grace during those years). My goal was simply to saturate my mind, heart and soul with His Word, even if it meant being subjected to statements like *"You're so intense!"* on occasion by both Believers and non-believers. But what I find truly amazing is that – regardless of my initial motivation – God still used the Pharisee-like rituals that I implemented for good.

His Word always delivers results.[9]

And His motivation?

It's always love.

I don't believe that God caused the cancerous cells, because He has no evil in Him.[10] But He did know that they were coming. And exactly when they would mount a full-on assault. So I have to smile realizing that He graciously prepared me for such a time as this...

Starting way back in my master bedroom closet.

Today, I listen more to a wide range of faith-based artists from Switchfoot and NEEDTOBREATHE to Hillsong United and Hollyn.[11] Our family has giggled with the Skit Guys via their website, laughed out loud to Tim Hawkins videos, and attended Christian concerts in our area.[12] I print out Bible verses accompanied by encouraging images from the Internet and mount them on bulletin boards throughout the house. We read the Bible at night, but instead of being feeling restricted to what others say is right, our family lets the Lord lead. Currently, the kids are going solo with their Bible time. But in the past, we'd often choose fun devotionals like "Get a Clue: The Case of the Howling Dog and 51 More Mysteries" or graphic novel Bibles.[13]

I still meet with the Lord every morning. But now I find myself wanting to reach out beyond the sunrise hours... reading Proverbs occasionally at lunch... praying for the kids and Mike on the way to and from school... and lifting my Facebook friends up to the Lord (even when there is no prayer request). I guess, for the first time in my life, I'm letting the Lord lead in terms of how He would like our *relationship* to be.

And isn't that what it's all about?

Jesus and me (or you).

Lately, it appears as though a few changes in the Huether's schedule may make the 4 AM routine a little difficult. Perhaps even impossible. Will I stray from my unwavering commitment to get together for meaningful conversation with my Savior?

NO WAY.

Not because I'm going to wake up at 3 AM every day! Even to me, that sounds crazy... especially since my 50+ year-old mind is already showing signs of losing it. I'm pretty confident that level of sleep deprivation would seal the insanity deal. Instead, I'm going to pray in confidence that Jesus will lead me to a new way and time to connect with Him that's even better than before.

But for now, I'm headed to the guest room, where I'll shut the door. Say a little Amen. Crawl under the table. And dive into some 1 Corinthians.

Because Jesus?

You're totally worth it.

---

1. For a child is born to us, a son is given to us. The government will rest on his shoulders. And he will be called: Wonderful Counselor, Mighty God, Everlasting Father, Prince of Peace. Isaiah 9:6 (NLT)

2. For I am not ashamed of this Good News about Christ. It is the power of God at work, saving everyone who believes. Romans 1:16a (NLT)

3. Stay alert! Watch out for your great enemy, the devil. He prowls around like a roaring lion, looking for someone to devour. Stand firm against him, and be strong in your faith. Remember that your family of believers all over the world is going through the same kind of suffering you are. 1 Peter 5:8-9 (NLT)

4. You prepare a feast for me in the presence of my enemies. You honor me by anointing my head with oil. My cup overflows with blessings. Psalm 23:5 (NLT)

5. Fix your thoughts on what is true, and honorable, and right, and pure, and lovely, and admirable. Think about things that are excellent and worthy of praise. Philippians 4:8 (NLT)

6. https://www.navigators.org/resource/topical-memory-system/

7. *The Hide the Word* series is available from Forever Grateful Music: http://www.forevergratefulmusic.com. *God Rocks!* is Christian band based on the award-winning kids' animation series of the same name. "God Rocks" CDs may be available from Amazon third-party sellers.

8. I will sing of the Lord's unfailing love forever! Young and old will hear of your faithfulness. Psalm 89:1 (NLT)

9. Oh, the joys of those who do not follow the advice of the wicked, or stand around with sinners, or join in with mockers. But they delight in the law of the Lord, meditating on it day and night. Psalm 1:1-2 (NLT)

10. This is the message we heard from Jesus and now declare to you: God is light, and there is no darkness in him at all. 1 John 1:5 (NLT)

11. https://switchfoot.com, https://www.needtobreathe.com, https://hillsong.com/united/, https://www.iamhollyn.com

12. https://skitguys.com, https://timhawkins.net

13. "Get a Clue: The Case of the Howling Dog and 51 More Mysteries" by Mark R. Littleton may available from Amazon third-party sellers. Looking for graphic novel Bibles? The "Action Bible" may be a great place to start: https://www.theactionbible.com

OPERATION
PB&J

Our family just got smacked with a jaw-dropping bill. Following on the goliath heels of this financial surprise, our furnace decided to go rouge. We are awaiting final word on the repair, which is estimated to be $1,500 or more.

Funny how these recent life developments came within 48 hours after I received official word from the surgeon's office that my abnormal cells were not cancerous.

So what do I do with all of this?

That is, besides run to Sams Club® for a wholesale-size case of Skippy Peanut Butter® and a few loaves of bread as our family's main dinner entree for the next 12 months.

I remember reflecting shortly after the surgery, during one of my Quiet Times with Jesus, how strange to be taken from the mountain of spiritual intimacy with the Creator of the Universe to the same-old's of "To-Do's" and sibling conflicts.

When cancer was dangling in front of me daily, I had to fling myself completely at His feet, in total submission and utter dependence. It was the only way to overcome the tremendous temptations that threatened to hammer my heart, soul and mind during a potentially life-alternating medical diagnosis.

It was scary at times, yes.

But, oh, did that place feel good.

And I miss it.

Of course, I do not miss the possibility of cancer! Instead, I long for the out-of-this-world, indescribable bliss of feeling totally and helplessly embraced in the arms of my Savior nearly every moment of every day.

When I wrote that big check yesterday, it dug up some pretty nasty past insecurities from my 40+ years prior to knowing Jesus. (I'm a latecomer to the Christianity scene.) As I attempted to squeeze all those numbers into that tiny green space, it reminded me of the seriousness of our financial situation – and caused me to readdress that tired-old question that threatened to rear its ugly head once again.

Is Jesus enough?

Will the Prince of Peace keep this family's money manager in a mental state that will successfully combat her tendency for fear and anxiousness, which could – I know from past experience – spread like wildfire throughout our home?

Well, this morning, like usual, my Savior didn't get down me for teetering on the edge of trust. No screams of condemnation: HOW CAN YOU DOUBT ME AFTER ALL THAT I'VE DONE? *(All caps? Harsh tone of voice? Those are sure signs of an Enemy attack, Sisters!)* Nor did He kick me to the spiritual curb for wandering on the fringes of worry. Instead, Jesus stood by His unshakable promise of no-matter-what Love. He even blessed me with some enlightenment via His Word.

Courtesy of Psalm 121.

Like so many Quiet Times before, I did not initially set my sights on reading this particular piece of Scripture. I have my own daily Bible reading plan, thank you! Yet as I sat down intent on delving into MY plan, Jesus once again graciously led me to a precious A-ha moment that comes from not only spending time in His Word, but also allowing HIM to take the lead in our morning dance.

As I read through Psalm 121, Jesus took me back in time and revealed how He walked alongside me during my college years... when I slept on a twin-size mattress the consistency of a marsh-mallow temporarily borrowed from a friend... stored my books in milk crates lifted (ok, stolen, let's call it like it is) from the local supermarket's back lot at 2AM... and listened to tunes on the $1 record player that I purchased at Goodwill®. My college was funded in part by scholarships, grants, two part-time jobs and twice-weekly plasma donations.

I look up to the mountains — does my help come from there?
My help comes from the Lord, who made heaven and earth.[1]

I can see how Jesus never left my side, even in the early years of our marriage, as I sat alone in front of the computer screen... looking at figures that just didn't add up... and wondering how Mike and I were going to pay for our housing, food and gas on the entry-level salary of woman with a Bachelor's degree in Jour-nalism employed at a non-profit organization and her hubby's grad student stipend of less than $2,000 per year. I recall the days when the money to fuel our good-ol' "Blue Comet" often came from deep within the folds of a hand-me-down couch – and the disgusted look from the convenience store clerk when we clunked coins on the counter. I wanted to yell, "Seriously, dude, we're not trying to be funny or cruel!"

He will not let me stumble;
the one who watches over me will not slumber.[2]

I can see that Jesus stood beside me, as Mike graduated and we began the long process of paying off student loans and "establishing" ourselves. Choosing a house outside our comfort zone of affordability, because we thought it may have the best resale value. (Mike's industry is notoriously known for company buyouts and relocations). Purchasing a second vehicle and, minutes before signing the papers at the auto dealer, discovering the numbers that I crunched were incorrect – and the monthly payments were several hundred dollars more than we anticipated or could afford.

Indeed, He who watches over me never slumbers or sleeps.[3]

I can see Jesus listened to cries of both celebration and concern, as we welcomed another family member – our son Chase – into the financial chaos. Wondering how we could ever send this little guy to college and "secure" his future. Signing up Chase to attend a private Christian preschool, only because it seemed refreshingly different than any other academic setting that we screened in terms of "We really do care about your son, this is not just a pre-admission show." Then discovering before the start of my son's second school year that we were far short from the amount of money needed to pay tuition.

The Lord himself watches over me![4]

I can see that as I chose to ignore Him all those years, I suffered the consequences of that stubbornness. My mental health was tormented by the fact that a statistically-clueless woman was steering her family down a rocky we-have-no-budget path... floating through each day... not knowing if we'd have the money to cover any inevitable disaster strikes. Why didn't I share this burden with Mike? I might have, but likely – without the wise counsel of the Holy Spirit living inside me – I expressed concerns with my hubby via irritability, blaming and resentment. "It's your fault, not mine!" is not exactly the moniker for contentment, either from a financial or matrimonial point of view. (Looks like He protected my marriage, too!)

The Lord stands beside me as my protective shade. The sun will not harm me by day, nor the moon at night.[5]

I can see that only by trusting Jesus could the chains of insecurity, fear and hopelessness be broken – and removed permanently. Since I've come to know the Lord as my Savior, our family has experienced more prosperous times financially. We've paid off the student loans. Eliminated most of our debt, with the exception of our mortgage. And stopped using credit cards as a means for day-to-day survival.

Not so long ago, we even managed to set aside some savings for the first time in Huether history. Oh well, at least I enjoyed a little taste that I finally had this budget thing down. Remarkably, the hefty bill is the exact dollar amount in our savings account! Sure, I could be bummed out. Or if I truly believe that the Lord always goes before me, I could definitely say that He enabled this money-illiterate mama to stash the perfect amount of cash for precisely this reason.

For such a time as this.

Don't get me wrong: I'm definitely not taking credit for any of this progress! And I certainly am not implying that my coming to know Jesus as my Savior – and what I do in obedience now – earns any favor from Him either in the dailies or in terms of my eternal salvation.[6]

Psalm 121 has provided me with eyes to see that God was there all along through every unintentional bad check. Every swipe of a credit card, often used as a last-ditch resort to purchase staples like food and shampoo. For most of my life, I was an overwhelmed in-over-my-head perfectionist – a two-times math flunky both in high school and college. Yet all along the way, God followed through with His divine plan for miraculously sustaining the Huether crew.

Today, I continue to remain clueless in the area of finances. Hey, numbers are just not my gift! But I'm a better wife to my husband. And a better mom to my children. Why? I have finally found the peace of knowing that I'll be just fine, whether He returns me to marshmallow mattress days or supplies just enough money to retire with my hubby on this 20 acres of God's natural wonder. (I just looked up briefly to find two young deer about 30 yards away from my chair out here on the front porch chasing each other playfully in the field. Nice touch, Jesus.)

Plus I'm, at least at this point in my life, cancer-free.

So how will I handle mini panic attacks that threaten me?

It's quite simple.

Psalm 121 shares a truth that I can grab hold of both today and in the Ramen noodle days to come. Despite my circumstances... material losses and gains... emotional highs and lows... the one thing that is 100% unchangeable is Jesus' love. Over 2,000 years ago, He paid off all my debt. That would be the countless wrongs that I willfully committed against God and others. (Those stolen milk crates, bad checks and marital blame games? Just microscopic specks on this woman's proverbial iceberg of sins.) Crazy thing? His one-time-for-all payoff covers my future mistakes, too! His sacrificial death and resurrection also guarantees a mortgage-free home with Him forever in heaven – one that is far more spectacular than the deer-dotted landscape that I see from the front porch of the country home that He's given me to steward, temporarily.

The Lord keeps me from all harm and watches over my life.[7]

I can see, after this morning's one-on-one with Jesus, the

Lord is not only watching over our finances but every detail of my life. Don't get me wrong; this "Whoa, baby!" bill is no small chuck of change. And yes, it definitely stirred up old fears! But I'm going to give all worries to the Lord – knowing without doubt that He's in control and loves me.[8] I am thankful that He blessed me with a mental trip through my past, present and future. Because no matter what life throws at me, I can say with confidence:

JESUS IS ENOUGH.

So bring on the furnace bill! (Ok, maybe I don't want to get that crazy.) And hospital bills from the past month's medical procedures, which will start creeping their way into our tank-sized, industrial-strength country mailbox. (Why is this thing so big? Maybe I'll throw that question at Jesus tomorrow morning.) Nevertheless, I will continue to trust that my Savior will keep me spiritually camped out in the heavenly reality of His presence and protection – even when my earthly view would tempt me to think otherwise.

The Lord keeps watch over you as you come and go, both now and forever.[9]

He's going to arm me with everything I need, as I continue to consult with Him daily through the Bible and pray without ceasing. I'm going to call it, "Operation PB&J." (That would be Peanut Butter & Jesus.)

What the heck!

I'm feeling celebratory.

Let's throw some ground beef in that shopping cart.

———————————————

1. Psalm 121:1-2 (NLT)
2. Psalm 121:3-4 (NLT)

3. Psalm 121:4 (NLT)
4. Psalm 121:5a (NLT)
5. Psalm 121:5b-6 (NLT)
6. God saved you by his grace when you believed. And you can't take credit for this; it is a gift from God. Salvation is not a reward for the good things we have done, so none of us can boast about it. Ephesians 2:8-9 (NLT)
7. Psalm 121:7 (NLT)
8. Give your burdens to the Lord, and he will take care of you. He will not permit the godly to slip and fall. Psalm 55:22 (NLT)
9. Psalm 121:8 (NLT)

GET REAL

Music & Cowpies

H*mmm...*
Better walk the dogs right away today, I thought, as our mud-caked Honda Pilot rolled into the gravel driveway... heading towards the garage with the door already raising up. Now 8:13AM, I was just returning home from dropping off the kids at school. The temperature gauge on my vehicle's dashboard displayed 68 degrees. The forecast called for an afternoon high in the mid-80's.

My "To-Do" engine was off and running. I started a load of laundry and added a few line items to my list – like rescheduling haircut appointments and mailing the check to pay our income taxes. (Yes, I've been procrastinating on that one.) I then headed into our mudroom to retrieve the dog leashes from the closet.

I stepped outside to marinate myself with the perfume of country life: Deep Woods Off®. Ticks not only run rampant in these-here parts, I suspect those pests hold daily meetings down near the corn crib to discuss how many of them can gang up on a Huether leg in a 24-hour period. The record to date is 12 – a number that has equally reigned on both human and dog limbs.

I'm sensing a TMI right here.

I removed the Invisible Fence® collars from our dogs, then looped on their harnesses. I have good reason to resort to greater restraint; Redd and Hummer kick into predatory mode as soon as they venture out beyond their safe zone, i.e. underground wire that keeps them from wandering beyond the perimeter of our yard.

I love our country strolls, despite the fact that my arms have grown at least two inches since our move from the suburbs, thanks to the intrinsic pull of two Siberian Huskies. From Redd and Hummer's perspectives, I'm guessing that our lush acreage is a canine rendition of Disneyland®, loaded with natural entertainment options. Free from the restrictions of sidewalks and property lines, my pups rollercoaster back and forth across the gravel road, happily riding the knee-high grassy shoulders. Figuratively and literally, they are digging their new home, rustling up field mice, pheasants and other wildlife.

I grabbed my cell, ear buds and keys.

Then the three of us headed out the door.

~

Before taking off down the wooded trail, I stopped to admire the endless sky swirled with milky blues and swooping landscape dotted with green hues. Honestly, every day, starting the moment that I lift up the window shades and enjoy a blast of purple-glazed sunrise, I thank the Creator of the Universe for blessing me with this sublime artistry that could never be recreated or captured by any human on canvas.[1]

It helps me keep everything in perspective.

His perspective, that is.

Just a few steps beyond "civilization" (a.k.a., our house, but I lovingly use the term loosely), I am surrounded by the intoxicating aroma of wild lilacs, sprinkled all over the countryside.

Last summer, I didn't notice these slender violet beauties during the three U-Haul trips that marked our transition from city to country life. Today, just a few days shy of our first anniversary on this 20-acre wonderland, I'm soaking up all the glorious details!

As I attempted to pull back the reins on two very anxious-to-be-walked dogs, I wrestled with slipping in my ear buds. As I fumbled, I found myself pausing once again. I heard a don't-miss-this choir of birds singing what I sensed was a live-in-the-moment melody. I stuffed the ear buds deep into one of my pockets. God seemed to be sending a clear message that – at least for today – it was time to set aside The Biopsy Playlist.

Over the past couple of months, this iTunes® playlist had proven to be one of my most effective spiritual weapons against worry, stress and the dreaded "what if's." (Daily Bible time and prayer will always rank as my #1 go-to's.)

It includes just four songs:

- "One of These Days" (FFH)
- "Hanging by a Moment" (Lifehouse)
- "Shake" (MercyMe)
- "Thank You" (33 Miles)

On April 1st, after returning home from the "this looks suspicious" mammogram, God prompted me to create my first-ever playlist. I had listened to music on my iPhone before. But up to this point, I simply had no desire to use the playlist feature – despite the fact that the Huether's iTune library encompasses 1000's of selections, both Christian and secular, thanks to living with two young musicians. Strangely, I recall no rhyme or reason as to why I chose these four songs. I like these artists. I just wouldn't consider these tunes to be among my all-time favorites (although they certainly hold a sweet spot in my heart now, that's for sure!)

I vividly recall that – right after the playlist was created – I rushed outdoors and was immediately comforted listening to the melodies, while surrounded by the peaceful solace of our secluded acreage. From that day forward, I listened to these four songs every day while walking my dogs.

But, oh, I wouldn't just play them.

I would shout out the lyrics at a maximum volume that surprised but probably not delighted my vocal cords. I'd walk with my face pointed upwards towards the Heavens, trusting my faithful canines to keep us somewhat centered on the trail. Occasionally, I'd lift an outstretched arm to the sky – or at least as high as the dog leashes would allow me. (I've always wanted to raise my hands during Sunday church worship, but afraid my hubby and kiddos might retreat to under the pews.) Another possible reason the Lord moved us to the country? No neighbors to frighten away with the sights and sounds of this overzealous woman's jam sessions with Jesus.

I'd never experienced anything like this worship.

Interestingly, none of these songs seemed to convey a woe-is-me or praise-you-in-this-storm kind of theme. At least not to me. I sensed only contentment, gratitude and praise.

For 30 minutes every day, the playlist became my great escape into 100% focus on His perfect character and everlasting love. This musical Trust-in-the-Lord mindset helped me meditate on His iron-clad promise that, regardless of the medical diagnosis, it was a win-win situation for me. Either I would remain here on Earth and enjoy my family. Or I would be headed to eternal Paradise with Jesus.

On this particular morning, the Lord seemed to be telling me to hit the trails without my usual musical weapon in spiritual warfare. Maybe it was because I was recently deemed cancer-free? (However, I'll be seeing an oncologist for five years and taking anti-cancer meds. But no complaints, believe me!)

Whatever the reason, He was leading me to be "in tune," so to speak, with the joyful symphony of birds chirping... cool breeze sweeping across my checks... and warmth of the summer sun on my face.

All sounded good to me.

~

A mere 15 minutes into our walk, Hummer started to wander off the grassy trail that my husband and son so nicely mowed through the acreage. This retreat from the beaten path didn't seem too unusual; the oldest of our canine family members was known to occasionally veer off track to tackle a field mouse. I readied myself for an uncomfortable cram-my-hand-down-his-throat moment to dislodge any creature who could become Hummer's mid-afternoon snack.

Oh, the glamorous country life.

YIKES!

That's when I saw it.

A 4½ foot snake with a girth – I kid you not – as large as one of my thighs had apparently been rudely awakened from his morning nap. My two dogs were inches away from meeting face-to-face with this seemingly disgruntled neighbor. Instinctively, I yanked the dogs' leashes back, while the serpent began to curl up, as if readying himself for who-knows-what. He slowly lifted his head... backed it up slightly... then start spewing reptilian insults with a few rapid flicks of his forked tongue.

Clearly, he wasn't a member of the local Welcome Wagon®.[2]

My emotions alternated between moments of awe ("Wow, he's ginormous!") and terror ("Is he the only one?"). Next came stupidity. ("I've got to get a photo!") As the dogs' leashes coiled around my legs due to impatience, I wondered how to obtain a Kodak® moment without putting myself or canine kiddos in harm's way. I wasn't sure what kind of snake it was... or if he was poisonous. But I was convinced that I needed a photo on my cell phone or no one would believe me. I'm known in the Huether household as an enthusiastic storyteller who may elaborate exuberantly on a detail or two.

Really, it was 4½ feet long!!

So what's a photo-crazed mama to do?

Well, of course, I started flinging sun-dried cowpies that were laying around nearby. Duh! (Isn't that part of every wanna-get-your-attention-snake plan?) This ruse was intended to not only shoo him away, but also secure visual proof.

Or maybe I should I say "poo" him away.

∽

Did I get the goods?

Yup.

Upon my return home, I discovered the infamous reptilian run-in successfully recorded on my iPhone camera roll. However, in my haste to take the photo, while sparing myself and the dogs any biting memories, what I was able to capture in terms of imagery is somewhat of a blur. Literally. In other words, it wasn't quite enough evidence to solidify any this-woman-is-not-hallucinating deal. But it wasn't the snake in the grass that ended up giving me the most memorable image.

It was the one in my kitchen.

Every morning, before I close up my Bible, I like to google a verse from my time with Jesus that was particularly meaningful. I look not only for the verse, but also an interesting picture that goes with it. I print the verse+picture on cardstock. Then place it on a mini stand on our kitchen island. It's a great all-day reminder for a visual person, like me.

This morning's verse?[3]

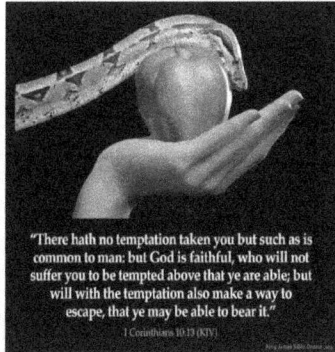

"There hath no temptation taken you but such as is common to man: but God is faithful, who will not suffer you to be tempted above that ye are able; but will with the temptation also make a way to escape, that ye may be able to bear it."

I Corinthians 10:13 (KJV)

I rarely post the KJV version of Bible verses. Although it's a fine version, no doubt, I usually choose one that is easy to read, especially for the younger members of the Huether clan. However, as I was wrapping up my Quiet Time with Jesus this AM, this KJV verse and imagery really spoke to me.[4]

I felt it was a perfect reminder that Jesus is faithful.

∾

So here I am, counter stool pulled up to kitchen island, staring at the snake in front of me. I'm happily typing on the computer... praising the Lord for bladder control... and wondering if I should break this latest "Welcome to country life!" news to my kiddos. (If I share it, though, I will likely lose the prospect for any future strolls down the Huether trail with human beings.)

I'm in awe of how the Lord goes before me.[5]

Earlier this spring... He led me to create The Biospy Playlist, which has served as a safeguard from the temptation to doubt His goodness. Although a seemingly small thing, this 30-minute spiritual groove proved HUGE in helping keep my faith and sanity intact – important not only to me as an individual, but also as wife and mama in the Huether house.[6] (If your family is like ours, when Mom is "out of commission," the entire team takes a serious hit!)

Earlier this afternoon... He led me to lose the music, at least for today's hike outside. By listening and following His prompting, I avoided wearing that viper as a shoe – and not a very fashionable one. One misstep on his slithery back could have potentially warranted a trip to the emergency vet. (Throwing two 50+ lb. Huskies in the back of a Honda Pilot for a 40-minute drive is not my idea of a good time.)

And just a little over one year ago... He led me to relocate from city to country. When we first pulled up and saw the "For Sale" sign, my omniscient God was clearly in control of every detail. He graciously chose to move me to this peaceful sanctuary... removing all distractions... so that I could grow closer to Him.

He knew the "big one" was coming.[7]

Essentially, the Lord was preparing for my victory over one of the biggest trials that I've ever experienced. Over the past year, He has strategically provided me with everything that I needed to not only survive but thrive in my faith, while I awaited the results from the pathologist. Ultimately, every time I follow His lead, I avoid the pitfalls, vices and temptations of choosing anything other than His perfect plan for my life. Scary but true: When I say "no" to Jesus, I say "yes" to the *very real* attacks from a *very real* Serpent whose mission is my destruction.

What evidence do I have to support this fact?

I know the Enemy full well.

I followed his worldly advice for 40+ years of my life – and ended up hurting not only myself, but everyone around me. I can only imagine what the past few weeks would have looked like... if I had tucked away my Bible in a drawer and opted for the opposite of God's perfect ways – as I used to habitually choose to do. Without doubt, I would have been stressing out vs.

celebrating all the blessings. Like the peaceful country life. Out-of-this-world music. And the joy of knowing this Truth:

Jesus has been walking with me all this time.

Both on the trail and every second of my life. He's been holding my hand every step of the way. The difference between the old and new me?

I am happily choosing to let Him lead.

～

S o I jokingly refer to my new friend as "anaconda."

But the reality is that there are dangers in this world beyond what my eyes can see. I am so thankful for every time that I listen to the Lord... recognize His 24/7 presence... and trust Jesus to safely lead me through this crazy world with my life secured in His loving grip.[8] Because I know that one day, when the door opens up to my heavenly home, I will not just sense His hand in mine.

His touch will be as real as my fingers on this keyboard.

Until then, I will continue my musical jam sessions with Jesus. Fling more cowpies, if needed. And pray that I'll never run short of a now-critical addition to future dog walks.

Hand sanitizer, please!

---

1. The heavens proclaim the glory of God. The skies display his craftsmanship. Psalm 19:1 (NLT)
2. https://welcomewagon.com/history/
3. Scripture quotation from The Authorized (King James) Version. Rights in the Authorized Version in the United Kingdom are vested in the Crown. Reproduced by permission of the Crown's patentee, Cambridge University Press.
4. https://www.kingjamesbibleonline.org/1-Corinthians-10-13_Inspirational_Image/

5. Do not be afraid or discouraged, for the Lord will personally go ahead of you. He will be with you; he will neither fail you nor abandon you. Deuteronomy 31:8 (NLT)

6. For the Lord your God is living among you. He is a mighty savior, He will take delight in you with gladness. With his love, he will calm all your fears. He will rejoice over you with joyful songs. Zephaniah 3:17 (NLT)

7. You saw me before I was born. Every day of my life was recorded in your book. Every moment was laid out before a single day had passed. Psalm 139:16 (NLT)

8. But let all who take refuge in you rejoice; let them sing joyful praises forever. Spread your protection over them, that all who love your name may be filled with joy. For you bless the godly, O Lord; you surround them with your shield of love. Psalm 5:11-12 (NLT)

I DO

Covenant Love

O h, He makes me chuckle.
  And smile.

Once again, the God of the Universe presents one of the most unlikely yet sovereignly wise remedies – at least for the time being – to prevent the reemergence of pre-cancerous cells that assaulted my body just two months ago.

Right now, I am gazing over at the earthly love of my life. My husband Mike is sitting beside me, outside on our deck under a partly overcast sky. We are surrounded by an amazing chorus of songbirds plus one baritone owl, who can be heard crooning from our corn crib several yards away.

Mike is scanning a cookbook recently borrowed from our local library for possible recipes to try out on our family. We are a household of picky eaters; Mike and I have yet to find one recipe that all four of us will eagerly eat at a single evening sit-down. It may be one of those issues that will never be resolved – or at least not until Chase and Mia reach 18 years old and are dining with the college crowd.

Or when Jesus returns.

Whichever comes first.

I tend to lean toward the likeliness of the latter.

But that wonderful husband of mine (and chef extraordinaire in our family's kitchen) is still going to give this seemingly mission impossible a try. He's not giving up, which is one of Mike's greatest gifts, and reason enough to thank God daily for compassionately placing this man in my life over 25 years ago.

But that's not what has me smiling.

I continue to remain in awe of the memory of Mike's whereabouts just a little over a week ago.

Mike was undergoing his own surgery.

He was stretched out on the operating table – less than one month after I made my appearance in St. E's hospital in that stylish polyester light-blue gown with the awkwardly open back.

The set of stitches that mark Mike's body right now don't stem from any physical ailment. His internal organs and cells – praise the Lord – are free and clear. His health is excellent, as far as we know. Any possible scars that Mike may show in the future are not the result of a must-have surgery, but rather a selfless offering of a husband to his wife in the spirit of covenant love.

Husbands, go all out in your love for your wives, exactly as Christ did for the church – a love marked by giving, not getting. Christ's love makes the church whole. His words evoke her beauty. Everything he does and says is designed to bring the best out of her, dressing her in dazzling white silk, radiant with holiness. And that is how husbands ought to love their wives. They're really doing themselves a favor – since they're already "one" in marriage.[1]

It's Ephesians 5:25-28, in the flesh (literally). I saw this verse play out for me so beautifully, over the past couple of weeks.

Thanks to the sweet man whom God chose to be my hubby. And a love marked by Mike's surprise giving.

~

"Stop taking your birth control pills, Chris."

Those were the words that matter-of-factly bolted out of my oncologist's mouth, as Mike and I sat in her office on Friday, June 6, which marked just a little over one month since my partial mastectomy. (Time flies when you're having fun, right?) Of course, the two of us responded with the utmost of calmness:

WHAT?!

I don't know whose lower jaw hit the floor faster, mine or Mike. Dr. T explained that high levels of estrogen had been shown to cause precancerous cell growth. If I stopped taking the Pill, it would be the first step – and perhaps only step needed – to help prevent the return of those types of cells.

Great?

My hesitancy arose from the fact that Mike and I have come to thoroughly enjoy intimacy together every morning.

You heard me right.

Every morning.

For years, Mike and I had quite different visions, in terms of frequency. Then I started hanging out with Jesus. And praying for my marriage daily. That's when the Lord convicted me that – instead of praying for changes in my husband – I should pray for changes in ME.

Ouch.

I hate when He does that!

Long story short, God revealed to me how His perspective on sex can take any marriage to a whole new level – both in and out of the bedroom. And not just for one person, but for the couple (yup, that includes me). Before putting His truths into practice, I was placing my own perceptions of what sexual intimacy means above the One who actually created this special marriage-only connection in the first place.

In God's perfect world, sex is reserved for a one-man-one-woman-for-life covenant relationship.[2] Covenant is this incredibly cool word for a loyalty unlike anything this world offers! In God's Kingdom, it's a promise that can't be broken. That's what makes God's covenant with His people, i.e. me and every Believer, so indescribably beyond-words wonderful. No other relationship can make that extraordinary I-love-you-forever claim. (Maybe that's why we don't hear the word "covenant" used much today.)

Marriage, when done right, is a close second.

So I decided to start wholeheartedly caring for Mike's physical needs, instead of just thinking of me. Essentially, I let go of the whole "I'm super tired" and "not in the mood" thing. I was holding back – and my marriage was not where it should be – because of my self-centeredness. *(Again, ouch, and Lord, why are you always right?!)* I began to pray for changes in (gulp) me. And I committed myself to spending time with my husband every morning after hanging out with Jesus in Quiet Time.[3]

Seven years later, our marriage has never been better! Many of the bliss-destroying influences once present in our lives are gone... from physical vices such as weekend drinking binges to destructive lies in my thought life, which were planted – no doubt – by the Adversary.[4] I totally get the fact that the Enemy of our souls is slyly working to destroy every God-ordained marriage. One of his attack strategies is fooling women into thinking that we don't desperately need that unlike-any-other, one-on-one time with our hubbies.

The Liar tries to convince us that it's just a guy thing.

BULL. (Can I say that biblically?)

In other words, God knows that He's doing! He's the Creator of the Universe. So it kind of makes sense, doesn't it? He's all about joy and fulfillment.[5] That includes sex in marriage. Just take 15-20 minutes today to read Song of Songs.[6]

Nuf said.

So when my oncologist proposed removing birth control pills from my life, well, it was a seemingly way-out-there-in-left field remedy – especially when sex is one of the areas that God has been beautifully using over the past few years for His glory – and Mike and my pleasure – to restore our marriage to everything it can and should be. I asked Dr. T how soon I needed to stop taking the Pill.

Immediately, she replied.

Huh?

I was speechless.

First of all, let me clarify that I ADORE children... and thank God every day that He brought two amazing people, i.e. son Chase and daughter Mia, into my life. But the thought of potentially giving birth to Baby #3 at the ½ century point of my life – well, that's a different story!

How can it be God's will for me to stop taking the Pill and switch to a possibly less-than-stellar birth control method... as my two current children are approaching the tail end of their habitation in our cozy nest... and Mike and I are nearing the last lap of punching our 8-5 clocks and looking ahead to retirement?

Whew!

Can you tell my mind at this point was a convoluted mess?

God has taught me to say, "Never say never," because His ways are not mine. Also, past history has shown that His ways are definitely preferable to mine.[7] In other words, Chris has a lot of really bad ideas. Looking back, I cringe considering "what if" He would have given me even a smidgen of what I thought was best over the past 50+ years? There is no font big enough for that "YIKES!"

But pregnancy in this season of my life?

At that moment in the oncologist's office, without time to reflect and temporarily too stunned to pray, that thought scared me almost more than the cancer! And I certainly did not want to give up, significantly reduce or add friction to the ever-growing intimacy with my hubby.

Then I heard Mike's voice cut through the thick silence.

"I'm getting a vasectomy," he said.

The three women in the room (me, the oncologist, and her assistant) all looked at Mike incredulously with eyes stretched to their widest. I blurted out, *"Oh, we should pray about that, hon... you don't have to do that...."* and other stuttering phrases to fill the not-sure-what-to-say airspace. My stammering was followed by remarks from the two female health providers in the room that never before had they heard any man so quickly offer up a surgical attack on his beloved buddies down below.

But Mike was insistent.

Two weeks later, my knight in shining armor was meeting with the urologist who – upon hearing Mike's sacrificial dedication to his previously pre-cancerous wife – waived the 6-8 week waiting period and scheduled Mike for a vasectomy by the end of the week.

∽

So this morning, Mike sits beside me on the porch with stitches inconspicuously hidden down below as we lounge in our lawn furniture. Sure, his stitches will dissolve within the next few days. The swelling is almost gone. Mike's delicate penguin-like walk and ice bag have been retired. The bruises are fading. But two very private places, under the surface, are forever marked by this husband's display of sacrificial love for his wife.

Jesus took the ugliness of my cancer (surely a tool of destruction from the Evil one) and continues to transformed it into something beautiful. First, Jesus used the cancer threat to draw me closer to Him. Now, He is using it to strengthen my marriage.

For His glory.

And my good.

I may not understand everything He does. But I know that, ultimately, by remaining steadfast in His Word and believing what He says is true, Jesus gives me eyes to see beyond our scars in this world. Enjoy glimpses of perhaps the deeper spiritual meaning within many of our hardships.[8] And live in gratitude knowing my Father in Heaven is perfect in every way – and perfectly loves all His children.

I consider my surgery (and Mike's) to be glorious proof.

But more glorious of all are the scars on Jesus' hands and feet. He sacrificed His life for you and me on the cross... then defeated the ultimate cancer – DEATH – as He was resurrected and ascended into Heaven. That's where all who believe in Him will meet as one big spiritual family... share our earthly scar stories... and triumphantly celebrate the following reality:

Every out-in-left-field had a divine purpose.

As I wrap up this chapter, Mike tells me that he's going into our house to unload the dishwasher. Afterwards, even with "his boys" still in a semi-fragile state, he plans to hike down to the corn crib and bring up wood for our fire pit. (Shh! Don't tell his urologist about this deviation from the master recovery plan.)

This is not the same man that I married.

And I'm not the same woman.

God is making us whole. Evoking beauty in our marriage. And bringing out the best in us. This covenant love thing? It all began when God invited me to experience the "WOW!" of a one-on-one relationship with his son Jesus.

I'm so thankful that I said "I do."

1. Ephesians 5:25-28 (MSG)
2. "Haven't you read," Jesus replied, "that at the beginning the Creator 'made them male and female,' and said, 'For this reason a man will leave his father and mother and be united to his wife, and the two will become one flesh'? So they are no longer two, but one flesh. Therefore what God has joined together, let no one separate." Matthew 19:4-6 (NIV)
3. It's good for a man to have a wife, and for a woman to have a husband. Sexual drives are strong, but marriage is strong enough to contain them and provide for a balanced and fulfilling sexual life in a world of sexual disorder. The marriage bed must be a place of mutuality—the husband seeking to satisfy his wife, the wife seeking to satisfy her husband. Marriage is not a place to "stand up for your rights." Marriage is a decision to serve the other, whether in bed or out. Abstaining from sex is permissible for a period of time if you both agree to it, and if it's for the purposes of prayer and fasting—but only for such times. Then come back together again. Satan has an ingenious way of tempting us when we least expect it. I'm not, understand, commanding these periods of abstinence—only providing my best counsel if you should choose them. 1 Corinthians 7:3b-6 (MSG)
4. Be sober-minded; be watchful. Your adversary the devil prowls around like a roaring lion, seeking someone to devour. 1 Peter 5:8 (ESV)
5. The thief's purpose is to steal and kill and destroy. My purpose is to give them a rich and satisfying life. John 10:10 (NLT)
6. Check out the following link for great introduction to this book of Bible, along with all eight chapters of the NASB version: https://bibleproject.com/explore/song-of-songs/
7. O Lord my God, you have performed many wonders for us. Your plans for us are too numerous to list. You have no equal. If I tried to recite all your wonderful deeds, I would never come to the end of them. Psalm 40:5 (NLT)
8. That is why we never give up. Though our bodies are dying, our spirits are being renewed every day. For our present troubles are small and won't last very long. Yet they produce for us a glory that vastly outweighs them and will last forever! So we don't look at the troubles we can see now; rather, we fix our gaze on things that cannot be seen. For the things we see now will soon be gone, but the things we cannot see will last forever. 2 Corinthians 4:16-18 (NLT)

EPILOGUE

Throughout my life, I've managed to pull off looking good. But the reality?

It was anything but pretty.

In high school, I was a nearly straight "A" student with an arguably impressive list of accolades, from newsletter editor and National Honor Society to vice president of the dance team and homecoming royalty. Believe me, there's no boasting here! Because, at least in my day, popularity was a dubious distinction. It included weekend binges on a wide range of illegal substances plus other "fun" activities played out either: (a) under the radar of unsuspecting parents or (b) with the blessing of "cool" moms and dads, who looked the other way or provided birth control, party kegs and don't-ask-don't-tell rides for drunk teens.

Kids will be kids!

Isn't that what the world says? I say it wasn't fun to be that kid when the party ended... waking up oblivious to the former night's debauchery, wearing someone else's T-shirt – and you had no clue who that someone else was – in addition to reeking like a distillery and suffering a hellacious hangover. And yet, it was the only life that I knew.

It's supposed to be like this, right?

A few years back, I ran into someone who informed me – much to my surprise – that we were in the same high school graduating class of 500+ students. Not only was I unaware of this fact, I discovered that – by staying "under the radar" – this woman also graduated with decent grades and an honorable list of achievements. However, she managed to avoid the hallmarks of so-called popularity: smoking, sex, drugs and alcohol.

My tradition of superficial goodness carried on through my college years: sorority president, Mortar Board member and State Capital intern by day; closet bulimic, party hopper and looking-for-'love'-in-all-the-wrong-places gal by weekend.

By the time I married my husband Mike, I maintained a façade of fitness by supplementing excessive cardio and weight-lifting with frequent trips to the toilet (courtesy of laxative abuse and an index finger carefully lodged down the throat). I held a full-time 40-hour-per-week job, while also piling freelance writing projects on the side without any regard to my sanity or physical health. This overtime helped pay the bills and mort-gage, while Mike worked on his doctoral thesis. Both high-achievers by nature, we spent what little time remained on the weekends partying with a small circle of friends with the same philosophy to life: Work your butt off during the week... then drown yourself in whatever substances are needed – from Friday at 6PM through Sunday – to escape from it all.

During those early years, my freelance business really took off. My portfolio looked good. I was gaining new clients every month. I boasted six-pack abs and 4% body fat. But underlying this "success" and drive for perfection came guilt, shame and regret. If that wasn't enough, anxiety and stress relentlessly suffocated me. Then entered the tsunami of worry:

My firstborn, Chase.

Unintentionally, I dragged my son into the madness of my

insecurities. Driven by an off-the-charts love that I had never experienced before for this tiny human being, motherhood was a mix of indescribable joy and mind-numbing fear. Unfortunately, the latter always seemed to reign victorious.

One evening of watching local news or reading *USA Today* had me wanting to leash my toddler. Safety harness, I believe, is the correct terminology. I had witnessed – and chuckled – when seeing parents "taking their kid for a walk" in busy airport terminals. (I think that's called being judgmental.) Now I was actually considering restraining my own son, as "what if" questions relentlessly haunted my thought life: *What if Chase is abducted? Or sexually molested?* The list went mercilessly on. (I'm realizing now I was the one who needed some restraining!)

My concerns quickly accelerated beyond the microcosm of the Huether world; the September 11 attacks occurred just 9 months into Chase's membership in this global community called Earth. We were living in Connecticut, which is a couple of hours from New York City. Mike was en route via plane to Brussels, Belgium. (Yup, he was one of those unfortunate few who were flying during the chaos.) It would be close to 48 hours before I discovered that his flight was rerouted to London and landed in Belgium safely. He was stranded there for nearly a week.)

After several hours of enduring the visual hysteria on T.V., I strapped on the baby sling, scooped Chase inside, and hightailed our asses (remember, I'm still a foul-mouthed mama in this season of life, LOL) to the local hardware store. We soon found ourselves stuck in the checkout lane – among the East Coast masses – with ungodly amounts of duct tape and industrial-sized rolls of plastic sheeting protruding from our shopping cart. Mom's biceps were swelling from pushing 100+ lbs of paranoia, in a mission to follow the government's advice on how to prepare for a potential terrorist attack. Basically, secure your home commando style! (I believe we still have a role in our basement, the sole survivor of a plastic battalion that – at one time – stood 20 rolls strong. It takes a lot of Saran® to wrap up a two-story Dutch Colonial.)

My former life was wracked with poor choices indicative of a woman who felt resigned to turn to herself for "wisdom" and direction. After being hurt too many times to count along the way, by way too many people, my self-imposed theology was that there was only one person that I could trust... only one person who could take care of herself (and her baby).

That person would be me.

An "every man for himself" mentality.

Today, my life has taken a 180° turn. I've dropped the pretentious I-can-do-it-myself-thank-you attitude. Lost the I-can-go-it-on-my-own mentality. And decided after years of human beings (including myself) letting me down, it was ok to finally trust someone. I just thoughtfully chose who that Someone would be. No, it's not my hubby, who I adore. Or my children, Chase and Mia, who are two of the greatest gifts that God has given me.

That someone else?

Jesus.

The name above all other names. The Savior of the world, not only the one that I see when looking out the window over our 20-acres of natural beauty... but also my small but precious world here in this home comprised of four imperfect people, two crazy canines, and a cat named Potato.

In this book, I've given just a glimpse of how Jesus not only rescued me from my former life, but gave me a new one – sweeter than anything I could have imagined. It's not free from bad choices. I still make a few now and then, but there's less, thanks to the times that I actually listen to the Holy Spirit. There are still painful circumstances outside of my control. And the news remains wrought with tragedy.

But as Song of Songs states so beautifully in verse 3:4:

I have found the One who my soul loves.

The One who died on the cross and took the blame for my selfish choices. The One who rose from the dead and offered me another way – the only way – to do this life right. The One who extended a free invite to come along for His glorious ride into Paradise (even when I don't deserve it). And the One who freed me from guilt, shame and regret – all the nastiness holding me back from being the woman that He created me to be.

Today, I am living in the joy of a redemption story.

Free from bulimia and this world's relentless lies about beauty. Free of alcohol and other false remedies for feeling good. Free from the insatiable drive to achieve success, always fighting but never living up to the world's standards. A former and recovering perfectionist, I'm finally enjoying the life that God always desired for me...

Perfectly beautiful.

Perfectly righteous.

Perfectly loved.

Perfectly in relationship with God, the Father and Creator of all things, through My Savior Jesus Christ. My prayer, in writing this book, is that you will experience it, too.

May you experience the love of Christ, though it is too great to understand fully. Then you will be made complete with all the fullness of life and power that comes from God.

— *EPHESIANS 3:19*

ABOUT THE AUTHOR

Chris Huether is a 30+ year veteran to the world of writing and a "first generation believer," which basically means she's clueless and clinging daily to the Word of Life.

After a successful career by society's standards as a freelance writer, she stepped out of the corporate world and into a sabbatical of sorts. She continued to dabble on the computer keyboard, joyfully writing pro bono projects for church, friends and family... until the Lord called her to publish these love stories.

Today, Chris resides in rural Nebraska with her family and a slew of critters, where she continues to revel daily in the never-ending grace and life-transforming power of the love of her life, Jesus.

www.ingramcontent.com/pod-product-compliance
Lightning Source LLC
Chambersburg PA
CBHW031700040426
42452CB00028B/600